THE CIVILIZATION OF THE AMERICAN INDIAN

THE SACRED PIPE

THE SACRED PIPE

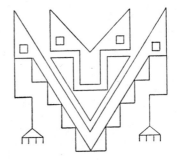

BLACK ELK'S ACCOUNT

OF THE SEVEN RITES OF THE OGLALA SIOUX

RECORDED & EDITED BY

JOSEPH EPES BROWN

NORMAN : UNIVERSITY OF OKLAHOMA PRESS

Library of Congress Catalog Card Number: 53-8810

Copyright © 1953 by the University of Oklahoma Press, Norman, Publishing Division
of the University of Oklahoma. Manufactured in the U.S.A. First edition, 1953; second
printing, 1967; third printing, 1970; fourth printing, 1971; fifth printing, 1975; sixth
printing, 1981.

To my people the Sioux

—BLACK ELK

Black Elk first became known to a wide range of readers in 1932 through John G. Neihardt's *Black Elk Speaks: The Life Story of a Holy Man of the Oglala Sioux*. Neihardt's poetic and sympathetic treatment of the old man's life and mission raised the question as to who, in fact, Black Elk really was. For if the account was faithful to only the essential qualities of the man, it was clear that even from a people noted for their large share of great personalities, here was an unusual man of vision; a holy man in the full sense of this term, and a man upon whom destiny, in a time of cultural crisis, had placed a heavy burden of responsibility for the spiritual welfare of his people. Here, also, could be an important message for the larger world.

I went to find Black Elk in the fall of 1947. After I had followed his traces across many of the Western states, we finally met in an old canvas wall tent on a Nebraska farm where his family and other members of their band were employed in harvesting potatoes. During that first encounter we simply sat side by side on a sheepskin, and silently smoked the red stone pipe which I had brought with me as an offering in the traditional manner. Partly crippled, almost completely blind, he seemed a pitiful old man as he sat there hunched over, dressed in poor, cast-off clothing. But the beauty of his face and the reverent quality of his movements as he smoked the pipe revealed that Neihardt had given to us the essence of the man, and the subsequent years spent with Black Elk have confirmed this initial impression. Knowing that Black Elk usually had refused to talk with many other people, it was with relief and wonder that I heard his first words: he had anticipated my coming, and wished me to spend that winter with him, for he had much to tell of the sacred things before they all should pass away.

I lived that very cold winter with Black Elk and his generous family in their little hewn-log house under the pine-covered bluffs near Manderson, South Dakota. Everything the old man told me I recorded in the time available when we were not hunting for wild game, or hauling water from the nearest hand-pump eight miles away, or cutting hardwood in the valley bottom for the iron stove, and I profited from this rigorous life which his family and my many new relatives shared with me.

I am fortunate in having met at least some of those men of the old days who possessed great human and spiritual qualities. But Black Elk had a special quality of power and kindliness and a sense of mission that was unique, and I am sure it was recognized by all who had the opportunity of knowing him.

According to his account, Black Elk was born in 1862. Therefore he had known the times when his people still had the freedom of the plains and hunted the bison; he had fought against the white men at the Little Big Horn and on Wounded Knee Creek. He was a cousin to the famous chief and holy man, Crazy Horse, and had known Sitting Bull, Red Cloud, and American Horse. Although Black Elk spoke no English, he had observed much of the white man's world, having traveled with Buffalo Bill to Italy, France, and England, where he danced for Queen Victoria—

"Grandmother England." But whether hunting, traveling, or fighting, Black Elk was not as other men are. During his youth he had been instructed in the sacred lore of his people by the great men, among whom were Whirlwind Chaser, Black Road, and the sage Elk Head, Keeper of the Sacred Pipe, from whom he learned the history and meanings of his people's spiritual heritage. With this understanding Black Elk prayed and fasted at length, until he himself became one of the wise men, receiving many visions through which he gained special powers to be used for the good of his nation.

This responsibility to "bring to life the flowering tree of his people" haunted Black Elk all his life and caused him much suffering. Although he had been given the power to lead his people in the ways of his grandfathers, he did not understand by what means the vision could be fulfilled. It was certainly due to this pervasive sense of mission that Black Elk wished to make this book, explaining the major rites of the Oglala Sioux, in the hope that in this manner his own people, as well as the white men, would gain a better understanding of the truths of their Indian traditions.

It has now been more than twenty years since Black Elk last spoke, and there have occurred many changes which demand that his message—and, indeed, similar messages of other traditionally oriented peoples—be placed in new perspective and in a new light. At the time when Black Elk was lamenting the broken hoop of his people's nation, it was generally believed, even by the specialists, that it would be only a matter of time—very little time in fact— until the Indians, with their seemingly archaic and anachronistic cultures, would be completely assimilated into a larger American society which was convinced of its superiority and the validity of its goals.

We are still very far from being aware of the dimensions and ramifications of our ethnocentric illusions. Nevertheless, by the very nature of things we are now forced to undergo a process of intense self-examination; to engage in a serious re-evaluation of the premises and orientations of our society. The inescapable reality of the ecological crisis, for example, has shattered for many a kind of dream world, and has forced us not only to seek immediate solutions to the kinds of problems which a highly developed technology has fostered, but also, and above all, to look to our basic values concerning life and the nature and destiny of man. The new generations today may not as yet be sure of the most effective means by which to further this process of re-evaluation, but many are looking with sincerity to the kinds of models which are represented by the American Indians.

In their relationships to this troubled America, Indian groups are seen to be situated across a wide spectrum of positions. On the one hand are the few traditional and conservative groups which, against enormous pressures, have miraculously remained very close to the essence of their ancient and still viable life-ways; and on the other hand are those groups which have been completely assimilated within the larger American society. Yet today, virtually all Indian groups who retain any degree of self-identity are now also re-evaluating, and giving positive valuation to, the fundamental premises of their own traditional cultures. They are also re-examining, through a wide range of means and expressions, their relationships to a larger society which today tends to represent diminishing attractions.

If there is validity to the above statements, it seems clear that it is too early to say that Black Elk's mission to bring his people back to "the good red road" has failed as he thought it had. Rather, it may be succeeding in ways which he could not have anticipated.

As an Oglala Sioux, Black Elk belonged to one of the seven sub-bands of the Western Teton, all of which speak the Lakota dialect of a Siouan language. These Western Teton are one of the seven bands, or "Seven Council Fires," of the Dakota (the "Allied"), which is one of the nations belonging to the large Siouan linguistic family. This linguistic group also includes the Assiniboin, Crow, Hidatsa, Iowa, Kansa, Mandan, Missouri, Omaha, Osage, Oto, Ponca, and Quapaw. According to the early history of the Dakota, they were established in the sixteenth century on the headwaters of the Mississippi, and in the seventeenth century they were driven westward from Minnesota by their enemies the Chippewa. In leaving the forests and lakes the Dakota substituted the horse for the bark canoe with remarkable ease, and in the nineteenth century they were known and feared as one of the most powerful nations of the prairies; indeed, it was these Dakota Sioux who offered perhaps the strongest resistance of all the Indian groups to the westward movement of the whites.

This account of the sacred pipe and the rites of the Sioux, was handed down orally by the former "keeper of the sacred pipe," Elk Head (*Hehaka Pa*), to three men. Of these three, Black Elk was the only one living at the time this history was written. (Black Elk died in August, 1950.) When Elk Head gave this account to Black Elk, he told him that it must be handed down. For as long as it is known, and for as long as the pipe is used, their people will live; but as soon as the pipe is forgotten, the people will be without a center and they will perish.

I wish to acknowledge my gratitude to Benjamin Black Elk, who acted as interpreter for this work and who is the son of Black Elk, to whom we owe this book. It is unusual to have an interpreter who understands both English and Lakota perfectly, and who is also familiar with the wisdom and rites of his people. I wish also to mention Benjamin's wife, Ellen Black Elk, a remarkable person of strong faith and character, who with quiet dignity always saw to it that everyone in her warm home was fed and cared for. Her death in September of 1970 was a loss for all who knew her.

I also acknowledge my gratitude to the Smithsonian Institution for the Barry photograph of Sitting Bull, and to the Illuminated Photo-Ad Service of Sioux Falls, South Dakota, who gave permission for the use of their photograph of the seven Sioux who participated in the battle of the Little Big Horn. These warriors were all close friends of Black Elk.

JOSEPH EPES BROWN

Bloomington, Indiana
February, 1971

TABLE OF CONTENTS

ILLUSTRATIONS

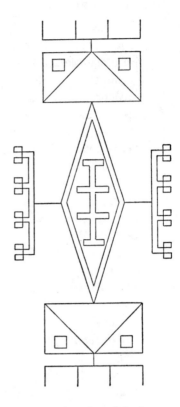

In the great vision which came to me in my youth, when I had
known only nine winters, there was something which has seemed
to me to be of greater and greater importance as the moons have
passed by. It is about our sacred pipe and its importance to our
people.

We have been told by the white men, or at least by those who
are Christian, that God sent to men His son, who would restore
order and peace upon the earth; and we have been told that Jesus
the Christ was crucified, but that he shall come again at the Last
Judgment, the end of this world or cycle. This I understand and
know that it is true, but the white men should know that for the
red people too, it was the will of *Wakan-Tanka,* the Great Spirit,
that an animal turn itself into a two-legged person in order to
bring the most holy pipe to His people; and we too were taught

that this White Buffalo Cow Woman who brought our sacred pipe will appear again at the end of this "world," a coming which we Indians know is now not very far off.

Most people call it a "peace pipe," yet now there is no peace on earth or even between neighbors, and I have been told that it has been a long time since there has been peace in the world. There is much talk of peace among the Christians, yet this is just talk. Perhaps it may be, and this is my prayer that, through our sacred pipe, and through this book in which I shall explain what our pipe really is, peace may come to those peoples who can understand, an understanding which must be of the heart and not of the head alone. Then they will realize that we Indians know the One true God, and that we pray to Him continually.

I have wished to make this book through no other desire than to help my people in understanding the greatness and truth of our own tradition, and also to help in bringing peace upon the earth, not only among men, but within men and between the whole of creation.

We should understand well that all things are the works of the Great Spirit. We should know that He is within all things: the trees, the grasses, the rivers, the mountains, and all the four-legged animals, and the winged peoples; and even more important, we should understand that He is also above all these things and peoples. When we do understand all this deeply in our hearts, then we will fear, and love, and know the Great Spirit, and then we will be and act and live as He intends.

BLACK ELK

Manderson, S. D.

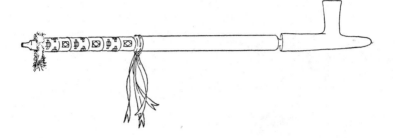

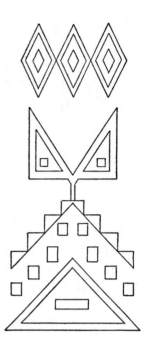

CHAPTER I

THE GIFT OF THE SACRED PIPE

Early one morning, very many winters ago, two Lakota were out hunting with their bows and arrows, and as they were standing on a hill looking for game, they saw in the distance something coming towards them in a very strange and wonderful manner. When this mysterious thing came nearer to them, they saw that it was a very beautiful woman, dressed in white buckskin, and bearing a bundle on her back. Now this woman was so good to look at that one of the Lakota had bad intentions and told his friend of his desire, but this good man said that he must not have such thoughts, for surely this is a *wakan* woman.[1] The mysterious person was now very close to the men, and then putting down her bundle, she asked the one with bad intentions to come over to her. As the

[1] Throughout this work I shall translate the Lakota word *wakan* as "holy" or "sacred," rather than as "power" or "powerful" as used by some

3

young man approached the mysterious woman, they were both covered by a great cloud, and soon when it lifted the sacred woman was standing there, and at her feet was the man with the bad thoughts who was now nothing but bones, and terrible snakes were eating him.[2]

"Behold what you see!" the strange woman said to the good man. "I am coming to your people and wish to talk with your chief *Hehlokecha Najin* [Standing Hollow Horn]. Return to him, and tell him to prepare a large tipi in which he should gather all his people, and make ready for my coming. I wish to tell you something of great importance!"

The young man then returned to the tipi of his chief, and told him all that had happened: that this *wakan* woman was coming to visit them and that they must all prepare. The chief, Standing Hollow Horn, then had several tipis taken down, and from them a great lodge was made as the sacred woman had instructed.[3] He sent out a crier to tell the people to put on their best buckskin clothes and to gather immediately in the lodge. The people were, of course, all very excited as they waited in the great lodge for the coming of the holy woman, and everybody was wondering where this mysterious woman came from and what it was that she wished to say.

Soon the young men who were watching for the coming of the *wakan* person announced that they saw something in the dis-

---

ethnologists. This latter term may be a true translation, yet is not really complete, for with the Sioux, and with all traditional peoples in general, the "power" (really the sacredness) of a being or a thing is in proportion to its nearness to its prototype; or better, it is in proportion to the ability of the object or act to reflect most directly the principle or principles which are in *Wakan-Tanka,* the Great Spirit, who is One.

[2] Black Elk emphasized that this should not only be taken as an event in time, but also as an eternal truth. "Any man," he said, "who is attached to the senses and to the things of this world, is one who lives in ignorance and is being consumed by the snakes which represent his own passions."

[3] The Sioux ceremonial lodge is constructed with twenty-eight poles. One of these poles is the "key," holding up all the others, and this pole the holy men say represents *Wakan-Tanka,* who sustains the universe, which is represented by the lodge as a whole.

4

tance approaching them in a beautiful manner, and then suddenly she entered the lodge, walked around sun-wise,[4] and stood in
front of Standing Hollow Horn.[5] She took from her back the
bundle, and holding it with both hands in front of the chief, said:
"Behold this and always love it! It is *lela wakan* [very sacred], and
you must treat it as such. No impure man should ever be allowed
to see it, for within this bundle there is a sacred pipe. With this you
will, during the winters to come, send your voices to *Wakan-Tanka,* your Father and Grandfather."[6]

After the mysterious woman said this, she took from the bundle
a pipe, and also a small round stone which she placed upon the
ground. Holding the pipe up with its stem to the heavens, she
said: "With this sacred pipe you will walk upon the Earth; for the

[4] The sun-wise or clockwise circumambulation is almost always used
by the Sioux; occasionally, however, the counter-clockwise movement is used
in a dance or some occasion prior to or after a great catastrophe, for this
movement is in imitation of the Thunder-beings who always act in an anti-
natural way and who come in a terrifying manner, often bringing destruction.

The reason for the sun-wise circumambulation was once explained by
Black Elk in this manner: "Is not the south the source of life, and does not
the flowering stick truly come from there? And does not man advance from
there toward the setting sun of his life? Then does he not approach the
colder north where the white hairs are? And does he not then arrive, if he
lives, at the source of light and understanding, which is the east? Then
does he not return to where he began, to his second childhood, there to
give back his life to all life, and his flesh to the earth whence it came? The
more you think about this, the more meaning you will see in it." (*Black
Elk Speaks,* recorded by John G. Neihardt).

[5] Standing Hollow Horn, as leader of his people, should be seated at
the west, the place of honor; for in sitting at the west of a tipi, one faces
the door, or east, from which comes the light, representing wisdom, and
this illumination a leader must always possess if he is to guide his people in
a sacred manner.

[6] *Wakan-Tanka* as Grandfather is the Great Spirit independent of manifestation, unqualified, unlimited, identical to the Christian Godhead, or to
the Hindu *Brahma-Nirguna*. *Wakan-Tanka* as Father is the Great Spirit
considered in relation to His manifestation, either as Creator, Preserver, or
Destroyer, identical to the Christian God, or to the Hindu *Brahma-Saguna*.

5

Earth is your Grandmother and Mother,[7] and She is sacred. Every step that is taken upon Her should be as a prayer. The bowl of this pipe is of red stone; it is the Earth. Carved in the stone and facing the center is this buffalo calf who represents all the four-leggeds[8] who live upon your Mother. The stem of the pipe is of wood, and this represents all that grows upon the Earth. And these twelve feathers which hang here where the stem fits into the bowl are from *Wanbli Galeshka,* the Spotted Eagle,[9] and they represent the eagle and all the wingeds of the air. All these peoples, and all the things of the universe, are joined to you who smoke the pipe—all send their voices to *Wakan-Tanka,* the Great Spirit.

[7] As in the distinction made within *Wakan-Tanka* between Grandfather and Father, so the Earth is considered under two aspects, that of Mother and Grandmother. The former is the earth considered as the producer of all growing forms, in act; whereas Grandmother refers to the ground or substance of all growing things—potentiality. This distinction is the same as that made by the Christian Scholastics between *natura naturans* and *natura naturata.*

[8] The buffalo was to the Sioux the most important of all four-legged animals, for it supplied their food, their clothing, and even their houses, which were made from the tanned hides. Because the buffalo contained all these things within himself, and for many other reasons, he was a natural symbol of the universe, the totality of all manifested forms. Everything is symbolically contained within this animal: the earth and all that grows from her, all animals, and even the two-legged peoples; and each specific part of the beast represents for the Indian, one of these "parts" of creation. Also the buffalo has four legs, and these represent the four ages which are an integral condition of creation.

[9] Since *Wanbli Galeshka* (the Spotted Eagle) flies the highest of all created creatures and sees everything, he is regarded as *Wakan-Tanka* under certain aspects. He is a solar bird, His feathers being regarded as rays of the sun, and when one is carried or worn by the Indian it represents, or rather *is,* the "Real Presence." In wearing the eagle-feathered "war-bonnet," the wearer actually becomes the eagle, which is to say that he identifies himself, his real Self, with *Wakan-Tanka.*

The Spotted Eagle corresponds exactly, in the Hindu tradition, to the *Buddhi,* which is the Intellect, or the formless and transcendant principle of all manifestation; further, the *Buddhi* is often expressed as being a ray directly emanating from the *Atma,* the spiritual sun.

From this it should be clear what is really being expressed in the often misunderstood Ghost Dance song: *"Wanbli galeshka wana ni he o who e,"* "The Spotted Eagle is coming to carry me away."

When you pray with this pipe, you pray for and with everything."

The *wakan* woman then touched the foot of the pipe to the round stone which lay upon the ground, and said: "With this pipe you will be bound to all your relatives: your Grandfather and Father, your Grandmother and Mother. This round rock, which is made of the same red stone as the bowl of the pipe, your Father *Wakan-Tanka* has also given to you. It is the Earth, your Grandmother and Mother, and it is where you will live and increase. This Earth which He has given to you is red, and the two-leggeds who live upon the Earth are red; and the Great Spirit has also given to you a red day, and a red road.[10] All of this is sacred and so do not forget! Every dawn as it comes is a holy event, and every day is holy, for the light comes from your Father *Wakan-Tanka;* and also you must always remember that the two-leggeds and all the other peoples who stand upon this earth are sacred and should be treated as such.

"From this time on, the holy pipe will stand upon this red Earth, and the two-leggeds will take the pipe and will send their voices to *Wakan-Tanka*. These seven circles[11] which you see on the stone have much meaning, for they represent the seven rites in which the pipe will be used. The first large circle represents the first rite which I shall give to you, and the other six circles represent the rites which will in time be revealed to you directly.[12] Stand-

[10] The "red road" is that which runs north and south and is the good or straight way, for to the Sioux the north is purity and the south is the source of life. This "red road" is thus similar to the Christian "straight and narrow way"; it is the vertical of the cross, or the *ec-cirata el-mustaqim* of the Islamic tradition.

On the other hand, there is the "blue" or "black road" of the Sioux, which runs east and west and which is the path of error and destruction. He who travels on this path is, Black Elk has said, "one who is distracted, who is ruled by his senses, and who lives for himself rather than for his people."

[11] The seven circles are arranged in this manner:

[12] According to Black Elk, two of these rites were known to the Sioux prior to the coming of the sacred Woman; these were the purification rites of the sweat lodge, and the *Hanblecheyapi* (crying for a vision); the ritual of the pipe was, however, now added to both of these.

ing Hollow Horn, be good to these gifts and to your people, for they are *wakan!* With this pipe the two-leggeds will increase, and there will come to them all that is good. From above *Wakan-Tanka* has given to you this sacred pipe, so that through it you may have knowledge. For this great gift you should always be grateful! But now before I leave I wish to give to you instructions for the first rite in which your people will use this pipe.

"It should be for you a sacred day when one of your people dies. You must then keep his soul[13] as I shall teach you, and through this you will gain much power; for if this soul is kept, it will increase in you your concern and love for your neighbor. So long as the person, in his soul, is kept with your people, through him you will be able to send your voice to *Wakan-Tanka.*[14]

"It should also be a sacred day when a soul is released and returns to its home, *Wakan-Tanka,* for on this day four women will be made holy, and they will in time bear children who will walk the path of life in a sacred manner, setting an example to your people. Behold Me, for it is I that they will take in their mouths, and it is through this that they will become *wakan.*

"He who keeps the soul of a person must be a good and pure

[13] In translating the Lakota word *wanagi,* I have used the term "soul" in preference to "spirit," which has been used by many ethnologists; I believe this term, understood in its scholastic Christian sense, to be more accurate, for what is kept and purified in this rite is really the totality of the psychic entities of the being, which, although localized within a particular gross form (usually the lock of hair), are really of a subtle nature, intermediate between the gross body and the pure spirit. At the same time it should always be remembered that it is the pure spirit, which is the presence of *Wakan-Tanka,* which is at the "center" of both the subtle and gross entities. The soul is thus kept in the manner to be described so that there may be a prolongation of the individual state and, thus, that the subtle or psychic part of the being may be purified, so that a virtual liberation will be achieved. This corresponds very closely to the Christian state of Purgatory. For further explanation of this important question, see René Guénon, *Man and His Becoming* (London, 1945).

[14] "It is good," Black Elk has said, "to have a reminder of death before us, for it helps us to understand the impermanence of life on this earth, and this understanding may aid us in preparing for our own death. He who is well prepared is he who knows that he is nothing compared with *Wakan-Tanka,* who is everything; then he knows that world which is real."

8

man, and he should use the pipe so that all the people, with the soul, will together send their voices to *Wakan-Tanka*. The fruit of your Mother the Earth and the fruit of all that bears will be blessed in this manner, and your people will then walk the path of life in a sacred way. Do not forget that *Wakan-Tanka* has given you seven days in which to send your voices to Him. So long as you remember this you will live; the rest you will know from *Wakan-Tanka* directly."

The sacred woman then started to leave the lodge, but turning again to Standing Hollow Horn, she said: "Behold this pipe! Always remember how sacred it is, and treat it as such, for it will take you to the end. Remember, in me there are four ages.[15] I am leaving now, but I shall look back upon your people in every age, and at the end I shall return."

Moving around the lodge in a sun-wise manner, the mysterious woman left, but after walking a short distance she looked back towards the people and sat down. When she rose the people were amazed to see that she had become a young red and brown buffalo calf. Then this calf walked farther, lay down, and rolled, looking back at the people, and when she got up she was a white buffalo. Again the white buffalo walked farther and rolled on the ground, becoming now a black buffalo. This buffalo then walked farther away from the people, stopped, and after bowing to each of the four quarters of the universe, disappeared over the hill.

[15] According to Siouan mythology, it is believed that at the beginning of the cycle a buffalo was placed at the west in order to hold back the waters. Every year this buffalo loses one hair, and every age he loses one leg. When all his hair and all four legs are gone, then the waters rush in once again, and the cycle comes to an end.

A striking parallel to this myth is found in the Hindu tradition, where it is the Bull *Dharma* (the divine law) who has four legs, each of which represents an age of the total cycle. During the course of these four ages (*yugas*) true spirituality becomes increasingly obscured, until the cycle (*manvantara*) closes with a catastrophe, after which the primordial spirituality is restored, and the cycle begins once again.

It is believed by both the American Indian and the Hindu that at the present time the buffalo or bull is on his last leg, and he is very nearly bald. Corresponding beliefs could be cited from many other traditions. See René Guénon, *The Crisis of the Modern World* (London, 1942).

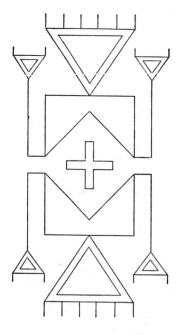

CHAPTER II

THE KEEPING OF THE SOUL

I

It is through this rite that we purify the souls of our dead, and that our love for one another is increased.[1] The four pure women who eat the sacred part of the buffalo,[2] as I shall describe, must always remember that their children will be *wakan* and thus should be raised in a sacred manner. The mother should sacrifice every-

[1] By an extraordinary act of either ignorance or ill will, this rite for the "keeping of the soul" was prohibited by the government in 1890, and it was even required that on a certain day, established by law, all souls kept by the Sioux must be released. For a description of this rite as performed in 1882, see Alice C. Fletcher, "The Shadow or Ghost Lodge," *Annual Report of the Peabody Museum,* Vol. III, Nos. 3, 4 (1884).

[2] The bison, which represents the universe, contains all things; but that part which represents mankind, and especially the holy White Buffalo Woman, is a certain meat from the shoulder of the animal. This meat is regarded by the Sioux in much the same way as is the holy Eucharist by the Christian.

thing for her children, and must develop in herself and in her children a great love for *Wakan-Tanka,* for in time these children will become holy people and leaders of the nation and will have the power to make others *wakan.* At first we kept only the souls of a few of our great leaders, but later we kept the souls of almost all good people.

By keeping a soul according to the proper rites, as given to us by the White Buffalo Cow Woman [known also as White Buffalo Maiden], one so purifies it that it and the Spirit become one, and it is thus able to return to the "place" where it was born—*Wakan-Tanka*—and need not wander about the earth as is the case with the souls of bad people; further, the keeping of a soul helps us to remember death and also *Wakan-Tanka,* who is above all dying.

Whenever a soul is kept, many of the nation go to its tipi to pray, and on the day that the soul is released all the people gather and send their voices to *Wakan-Tanka* through the soul which is to travel upon His sacred path. But now I shall explain to you how this rite was first done by our people.

One of the great-great-grandchildren of Standing Hollow Horn had a child whom the parents loved very much; but it happened that one day this child died, which made the father very sad, and so he went and spoke to the keeper of the sacred pipe, who was at that time High Hollow Horn.

"We have been instructed by the sacred woman in the use of the pipe and in the keeping of the soul of a person who has died. Now I am very sad because I have lost my loved son, but I wish to keep his soul as we have been taught, and, since you are the keeper of the sacred pipe, I wish you to instruct me!"

"*How! Hechetu alo!* It is good!" High Hollow Horn said, and they then went to the place where the child lay, and where the women were crying very bitterly. As they approached, the crying stopped; and going to where the child lay, High Hollow Horn spoke.

"This boy seems to be dead, yet he is not really, for we shall keep his soul among our people, and through this our children and the children of their children will become *wakan.* We shall now do as we were taught by the sacred woman and by the pipe. It is the wish of *Wakan-Tanka* that this be done."

A lock of the child's hair was then taken, and as High Hollow Horn did this he prayed.

"O *Wakan-Tanka* behold us! It is the first time that we do Thy will in this way, as You have taught us through the sacred woman. We will keep the soul of this child so that our Mother the Earth will bear fruit, and so that our children will walk the path of life in a sacred manner."

High Hollow Horn then prepared to purify the child's lock of hair; a glowing coal was brought in, and a pinch of sweet grass was placed upon it.

"O *Wakan-Tanka*," High Hollow Horn prayed, "this smoke from the sweet grass will rise up to You, and will spread throughout the universe; its fragrance will be known by the wingeds, the four-leggeds, and the two-leggeds, for we understand that we are all relatives; may all our brothers be tame and not fear us!"

High Hollow Horn took up the lock of hair, and holding it over the smoke, made a motion with it to Heaven, to Earth, and to the four quarters of the universe; then he spoke to the soul within the hair.

"Behold O soul! Where you dwell upon this earth will be a sacred place; this center will cause the people to be as *wakan* as you are. Our grandchildren will now walk the path of life with pure hearts, and with firm steps!"

After purifying the lock of hair in the smoke, High Hollow Horn turned to the mother and father of the child, saying: "We shall gain great knowledge from this soul which has here been purified. Be good to it and love it, for it is *wakan*. We are now fulfilling the will of *Wakan-Tanka*, as it was made known to us through the sacred woman; for do you not remember as she was leaving how she turned back the second time? This represents the keeping of the soul, which we are now going to do. May this help us to remember that all the fruits of the wingeds, the two-leggeds, and the four-leggeds, are really the gifts of *Wakan-Tanka*. They are all *wakan* and should be treated as such!"

Black Elk, 1947 *(Photograph by J. E. Brown)*

The lock of hair was wrapped in sacred buckskin, and this bundle was placed at a special place in the tipi. Then High Hollow Horn took up the pipe, and after holding it over the smoke, filled it carefully in a ritual manner; pointing the stem towards heaven, he prayed.

"Our Grandfather, *Wakan-Tanka,* You are everything, and yet above everything! You are first. You have always been. This soul that we are keeping will be at the center of the sacred hoop of this nation; through this center our children will have strong hearts, and they will walk the straight red path in a *wakan* manner.

"O *Wakan-Tanka,* You are the truth. The two-legged peoples who put their mouths to this pipe will become the truth itself; there will be in them nothing impure. Help us to walk the sacred path of life without difficulty, with our minds and hearts continually fixed on You!"

The pipe was then lighted and smoked, and was passed sunwise around the circle. The whole world within the pipe was offered up to *Wakan-Tanka.* When the pipe came back to High Hollow Horn, he rubbed sweet grass over it on the west, north, east, and south sides, in order to purify it lest any unworthy person might have touched it; turning to the people, he then said: "My relatives, this pipe is *wakan.* We all know that it cannot lie. No man who has within him any untruth may touch it to his mouth. Further, my relatives, our Father, *Wakan-Tanka,* has made His will known to us here on earth, and we must always do that which He wishes if we would walk the sacred path. This is the first time that we carry out this sacred rite of keeping the soul, and it will be of great benefit to our children and to their children's children! My relatives, Grandmother and Mother Earth, we are of earth, and belong to You. O Mother Earth from whom we receive our food, You care for our growth as do our own mothers. Every step that we take upon You should be done in a sacred manner; each step should be as a prayer. Remember this my relatives: that the power of this pure soul will be with you as you walk, for it, too, is the fruit of Mother Earth; it is as a seed, planted in your center, which will in time grow in your hearts, and cause our generations to walk in a *wakan* manner."

13

High Hollow Horn then lifted his hand and sent his voice to *Wakan-Tanka.*[3]

"O Father and Grandfather *Wakan-Tanka,* You are the source and end of everything. My Father *Wakan-Tanka,* You are the One who watches over and sustains all life. O my Grandmother, You are the earthly source of all existence! And Mother Earth, the fruits which You bear are the source of life for the earth peoples. You are always watching over Your fruits as does a mother. May the steps which we take in life upon you be sacred and not weak!

"Help us O *Wakan-Tanka* to walk the red path with firm steps. May we who are Your people stand in a *wakan* manner, pleasing to You! Give to us strength which comes from an understanding of Your powers! Because You have made Your will known to us, we will walk the path of life in holiness, bearing the love and knowledge of You in our hearts! For this and for everything we give thanks!"

A bundle was then made containing the body of the child, and the men took this to a high place away from the camp and placed it upon a scaffold set up in a tree.[4] When they returned, High Hollow Horn went into the tipi with the father of the child, in order to teach him how he must prepare himself for the great duty which he would fulfill and from which he would become a holy man.

"You are now keeping the soul of your own son," High Hollow Horn said, "who is not dead, but is with you. From now on you must live in a sacred manner, for your son will be in this tipi until his soul is released. You should remember that the habits which you establish during this period will remain with you always. You

[3] "We raise our hands (when we pray) because we are wholly dependent on the Great Spirit; it is His liberal hand that supplies all our wants. We strike the ground afterward, because we are miserable beings, worms crawling before His face." (As said by a Blackfoot Sioux to Father De Smet: *Life, Letters, and Travels* [New York, 1905], 253)

[4] It is in this manner that the gross body is given back to the elements from which it came; it is left exposed to the agents of heaven: the four winds, the rains, the wingeds of the air, each of which—and with the Earth—absorbs a part.

must take great care that no bad person enters the lodge where you keep the soul, and that there be no arguments or dissensions; there should always be harmony in your lodge, for all these things have an influence on the soul which is being purified here.

"Your hands are *wakan;* treat them as such! And your eyes are *wakan;* when you see your relatives and all things, see them in a sacred manner![5] Your mouth is *wakan,* and every word you say should reflect this holy state in which you are now living. You should raise your head often, looking up into the heavens. Whenever you eat of the fruit of Mother Earth, feed likewise your son! If you do this and all that I have taught you, *Wakan-Tanka* will be merciful to you. Every day and night your son will be with you; look after his soul all the time, for through this you will always remember *Wakan-Tanka.* From this day on you will be *wakan,* and as I have taught you, so you too will now be able to teach others. The sacred pipe will go a long way, even to the end, and so will the soul of your son! It is indeed so, *Hetchetu welo!*"

II

Before I tell you how the soul is released, I think I should explain several of the other duties which the keeper of a soul should know and should carry out.

He who keeps the soul of a person should never fight, or even use a knife, no matter for what purpose. He must be in prayer all

[5] The sacredness of relationship is one of the most important aspects of Siouan culture; for since the whole of creation is essentially One, all parts within the whole are related. Thus the Sioux refer to each other not by their particular names, but by a term expressing their relationship, which is determined by age levels rather than by blood ties. A young man thus always addresses an older man or woman as *"Ate"* (Father), or *"Ina"* (Mother), or if they are much older by: *"Tunkashila"* (Grandfather), or *"Unchi"* (Grandmother); and in turn the older address the younger as "Son" or "Daughter," "Grandson" or "Granddaughter."

For the Sioux, all relationships on earth are symbolic of the true and great relationship which always exists between man and the Great Spirit, or between man and Earth understood in its principle. In using these terms, the Sioux thus really invoke or recall the principle, and the individual—or really any particular thing—is for them only a dim reflection of this principle.

the time, and he must be an example to his people in everything. The people should love and honor this holy man, frequently bringing food and gifts to him, and the keeper of the soul should in turn offer up his pipe very often to *Wakan-Tanka* for the good of the nation.

When a party of warriors go on a hunt, the holy keeper of the soul should go with them, but while the others hunt, he should sit alone on a hill and with his pipe he should send his voice to the powers above for the good of the hunt and for the good of all the people. Then when a buffalo cow has been killed near the keeper, she belongs to him, and he should go and sit near her; then he should fill his pipe, by first offering pinches of *kinni-kinnik*[6] to the winged powers of the west, north, east, south, Mother Earth, and finally the last he should hold up, offering it to *Wakan-Tanka* in whom are all the powers. When the pipe has been filled in this manner, he should then point its stem towards the nose of the buffalo cow, and he should pray in this manner: "O *Wakan-Tanka*, You have taught us Your will through a four-legged one, so that Your people may walk the sacred path, and that our children, and our children's children, will be blessed. I am offering this pipe to You before all else, for You are always first, and then I offer it to *Tatanka* the buffalo.

"You O *Tatanka* have four ages, and the last time that you looked back upon us we saw that you are the fruit of our Mother Earth from whom we live. You will thus be the first to be placed at the center of our nation's hoop, for you strengthen our bodies and also our spirits when we treat you in a *wakan* manner. You have made known to us the will of *Wakan-Tanka,* so that now there is a holy soul at the center of our hoop. You will be at our center with this soul, and there you will give happiness to your people. Go now forward to the center of the people's hoop!"

[6] *Kinnikinnik,* often called *chanshasha,* is an ingredient of the tobacco of the Sioux; it is the dried inner bark of the red alder or the red dogwood (*Cornus stolonifera*). This is rarely smoked alone because of its bitterness; there is usually added to it an equal part of the Ree twist tobacco and also a small portion of some fragrant root or herb, often the Sweet Ann root. These ingredients are always mixed in a ritual manner.

Men who have been instructed by the keeper of the soul then butcher the *waķan* buffalo cow, saying appropriate prayers for every part. The meat taken from the shoulder represents the two-legged peoples, but especially the holy woman who brought the pipe to us; it is thus *lela waķan,* and is always treated with great respect. The keeper of the soul is not able to do any of the butchering since he can touch neither knife nor blood, as I have already mentioned; but he was able to take this *waķan* meat back to camp on his horse along with the buffalo hide, for this too is *waķan* and will be used for a special purpose. Their arrival at camp is announced by a crier, and the meat is then taken to the tipi of the keeper of the soul. At this moment one of the helpers within the lodge should speak to the soul.

"Grandson, the chosen food will rest at the center of this lodge, your home. It will be of great benefit to the people! *Hetchetu welo!"*

Within the tipi where a soul is kept, there should always be a woman who has been chosen to care for the sacred bundle; the first woman to fulfill this sacred duty was Red Day Woman. This holy person would sun-dry the *waķan* meat, and this would later be made into *wasna,* which is the dried meat (*papa*), pounded together with wild cherries and mixed with tallow taken from the bones of the buffalo. This sacred food is kept in a specially painted buffalo-hide box, and is saved for the day when the soul is released.

On good days the soul-bundle should be taken outside, and should be hung on a tripod, facing the south.[7] On these days the people often come to bring gifts to the soul, and to pray before it, thus gaining much benefit. These gifts also are kept in a specially

[7] The three feet of the tripod are oriented to the west, north, and east; it is thus left open to the south, which is, for the Sioux, the direction towards which the souls of the dead go. The sacred bundle is tied on the south side, just below the place where the three sticks intersect. This central point of intersection represents *Waķan-Tanķa* towards whom the soul will soon depart, and from this point there hangs a thong which just touches the ground, representing the way leading from the earth to *Waķan-Tanķa*. It is upon this way that the soul is now traveling, and the position of the bundle indicates that the journey has nearly been completed.

17

painted box, and they are later given away to the poor and needy.

After the buffalo robe has been tanned in a ritual manner, it is painted and is again purified over the smoke of the sweet grass. The keeper of the soul should then point this robe to the four quarters of the universe, and say: "O you soul, my grandson, stand firmly on this earth and look about you; look to the heavens, to the four quarters of the universe, and look upon your Mother the Earth! And you, O buffalo who are really here in this hide, you have come to our people to do them a great service; now you are to unite with this soul. You will both be at the center of the nation's hoop, and will represent the oneness of the people. By placing this robe over you, O soul, I am placing it over all the people as one."

When the sacred bundle is hanging from the tripod outside the lodge, this buffalo robe is placed over it with its hair on the outside, and on top of the tripod there should be placed a war bonnet, made from the feathers of *Wanbli Galeshka,* the Spotted Eagle.

Although the helpers are allowed to handle the equipment, only the holy keeper may touch the sacred bundle. This bundle he always carries against the heart, in the crook of the left arm, for this is the arm that is nearest to the heart, and whenever the bundle is taken back into the tipi it should be offered first to Heaven, then to Earth, and to the four directions of the universe.

Before the rites for the releasing of the soul can be made, many things must be gathered together, and for poor people this may take several years, but the usual length of time for keeping a soul is one year. Should the keeper die before the soul is released, then his wife keeps the soul, and also the soul of her husband; and should the wife die also, then the helpers keep all three souls, and this would of course be a very great and sacred responsibility.

Before the soul of the child is released, all the people gather to-gether, for everybody participates in this great rite, which can best be called The Making of Sacredness. As this time approaches, all the men go hunting for the buffalo, and when many are killed the bones are cracked and boiled, and from this tallow *wasna* is made. The women dry the best part of the meat, which is then called *papa,* and all this is contributed to the rites.

After first consulting with the other holy men of the band, the keeper of the soul—who was for this first rite a relative of Standing Hollow Horn—appoints the special day, and when this times arrives, the helpers make a large ceremonial lodge from sev-eral small tipis and cover the earth inside with sacred sage.

The helper of the keeper of the soul then takes a pipe, and holding it up to the heavens, he cries: "Behold, O *Wakan-Tanka!* We are now about to do Thy will. With all the sacred beings of the universe, we offer to You this pipe!"

The helper then takes a pinch of the sacred tobacco *kinni-kinnik,* and holding it and the stem of the pipe towards the west, he cries: "With this *wakan* tobacco, we place You in the pipe, O winged Power of the west. We are about to send our voices to *Wakan-Tanka,* and we wish You to help us!

"This day is *wakan* because a soul is to be released. All over the universe there will be happiness and rejoicing! O You sacred Power of the place where the sun goes down, it is a great thing we are doing in placing You in the pipe. Give to us for our rites one of the two sacred red and blue days which You control!"[8]

This Power of the west, now in the tobacco, is placed in the

[8] The term "red and blue days" is really far more than a wish for good weather, for the Sioux believe that these are the days at the end of the world when the moon will turn red and the sun will turn blue. But since for the traditional man everything in the macrocosm has its counterpart in the microcosm, there may also be an end of the world for the individual here and now, whenever he receives illumination or wisdom from *Wakan-Tanka,* so that his ego or ignorance dies, and he then lives continually in the Spirit.

pipe, and holding another pinch of *kinnikinnik* towards the north, the helper prays.

"O You, Thunder-being, there where *Waziah* has his lodge, who comes with the purifying winds, and who guards the health of the people; O Baldheaded Eagle of the north, Your wings never tire! There is a place for You too in this pipe, which will be offered to *Wakan-Tanka*. Help us, and give to us one of Your two sacred days!"

Then holding another pinch of *kinnikinnik* to the east, the helper continues to pray.

"O You sacred Being of the place where the sun comes up, who controls knowledge! Yours is the path of the rising sun which brings light into the world. Your name is *Huntka*, for You have wisdom and are long-winged. There is a place for You in the pipe; help us in sending our voice to *Wakan-Tanka!* Give to us Your sacred days!"

This Power of the east is placed in the pipe, and then another pinch of *kinnikinnik* is held towards the south, with the prayer: "O You who guard that path leading to the place towards which we always face, and upon which our generations walk, we are placing You in this sacred pipe! You control our life, and the lives of all the peoples of the universe. Everything that moves and all that is will send a voice to *Wakan-Tanka*. We have a place for You in the pipe; help us in sending our voice, and give to us one of Your good days! This we ask of You, O White Swan, there where we always face."

The stem of the pipe and a pinch of *kinnikinnik* are then held towards the earth.

"O You, sacred Earth, from whence we have come, You are humble, nourishing all things; we know that You are *wakan* and that with You we are all as relatives. Grandmother and Mother Earth who bear fruit, for You there is a place in this pipe. O Mother, may Your people walk the path of life, facing the strong winds! May we walk firmly upon You! May our steps not falter! We and all who move upon You are sending our voices to *Wakan-Tanka!* Help us! All together as one we cry: help us!"

When the pipe has thus been filled with all the Powers and
with all that there is in the universe,[9] it is given to the keeper of

[9] In filling a pipe, all space (represented by the offerings to the powers
of the six directions) and all things (represented by the grains of tobacco)
are contracted within a single point (the bowl or heart of the pipe), so
that the pipe contains, or really *is,* the universe. But since the pipe is the
universe, it is also man, and the one who fills a pipe should identify himself
with it, thus not only establishing the center of the universe, but also his
own center; he so "expands" that the six directions of space are actually
brought within himself. It is by this "expansion" that a man ceases to be a
part, a fragment, and becomes whole or holy; he shatters the illusion of
separateness.

In order to make clear this identity for the Indian of the body of man
with the pipe, I quote the following text of the Osage Indians:

These people had a pipe,
Which they made to be their body.

O *Hon-ga,* I have a pipe that I have made to be my body;
If you also make it to be your body,
You shall have a body that is free from all causes of death.

Behold the joint of the neck, they said,
That I have made to be the joint of my own neck.

Behold the mouth of the pipe,
That I have made to be my mouth.

Behold the right side of the pipe,
That I have made to be the right side of my body.

Behold the spine of the pipe,
That I have made to be my own spine.

Behold the left side of the pipe,
That I have made to be the left side of my own body.

Behold the hollow of the pipe,
That I have made to be the hollow of my own body.

Behold the thong that holds together the pipe and stem;
That I have made to be my windpipe.
. . . use the pipe as an offering in your supplications,
Your prayers shall be readily granted.

(Francis La Flesche, "War Ceremony and Peace Ceremony of the Osage
Indians," *Bulletin No. 101 of the Bureau of American Ethnology* [Wash-
ington, D. C., 1939], 62, 63)

the soul, who takes it and, crying as he walks, goes to the tipi of the keeper of the most sacred pipe, who was, for this first rite, High Hollow Horn. Entering the tipi, and holding out the pipe with its stem pointing towards the south, he places it in the hands of the keeper of the pipe.

"*Hi Ho! Hi Ho!* Thanks!" the holy man says as he takes the pipe, "this pipe which you have brought to me is really as sacred as the original pipe which was given to us by the White Buffalo Cow Woman. Indeed, to one who understands they are really the same. But this pipe which you have now brought is especially sacred, for I see that there has been placed within it the whole universe. What is it that you wish?"

"We wish you to smoke this pipe and then to lead the rites for releasing the soul of my young son. We wish you to bring with you the original *wakan* pipe which you are keeping."

"*How, hetchetu welo,*" the holy man replied, "I will come!" He then offers the pipe which has been brought to him to the heavens, to the earth, to the four quarters; then he smokes it. When finished, he carefully saves the ashes, for they too are very *wakan*.

The two men return to the lodge where all has been made ready for the great rite. Entering, they walk around sun-wise and sit at the west of the lodge, opposite the door. The wife of the keeper of the soul then goes to her tipi, crying as she walks, picks up the sacred bundle, and returns to the lodge, where she stands in front of the keeper of the sacred pipe, placing the bundle in his two outstretched hands. "Thanks, thanks!" the holy keeper says, and then he speaks to the soul within the bundle:

"You, O soul, were with your people, but soon you will leave. Today is your day, and it is *wakan*. Today your Father, *Wakan-Tanka,* is bending down to see you; all your people have arrived to be with you. All your relatives love you, and have taken good care of you. You and the holy woman of the four ages, who brought to us the sacred pipe, are now together here in this lodge; this robe here, which represents the sacred woman and which has covered you, will cover all your people! The sacred pipe which she brought to us has made the people happy. Behold! This is the sacred day! *Hetchetu welo!"*

A round circle is scraped on the ground to represent a buffalo wallow, and on this the sacred bundle is placed. Another round place is then made from the earth taken from the wallow, upon which a cross is drawn from west to east and from north to south. The pipe is placed upon this cross, with its stem to the west and the bowl at the east. Then the sacred bundle is placed beside the pipe, at the bottom of the good red road, for this is the place to which the soul will soon journey.

One of the helpers then goes to the fire at the center of the tipi and, with a split stick, picks up a glowing coal and places it in front of the keeper of the pipe.[10] The keeper then holds the pipe in his left hand, and, taking up a pinch of a sacred herb in his right hand, he holds it up towards the heavens and lowers it slowly to the coal, stopping four times and praying: "O Grandfather, *Wakan-Tanka,* on this sacred day of Yours, I send to You this fragrance, which will reach to the heavens above. Within this herb, there is the earth, this great island; within it is my Grandmother, my Mother, and all the four-leggeds, the wingeds, and the two-legged peoples, who are all walking in a *wakan* manner. The fragrance of this herb will cover the entire universe. O *Wakan-Tanka,* be merciful to all!"

The bowl of the pipe is placed over the smoke, in such a way that this smoke passes through the pipe, coming out the end of the stem which is held towards the heaven. In this manner, *Wakan-Tanka* is the first to smoke, and by this act the pipe is purified. As he does this, the "keeper of the pipe" prays.

[10] Since, for the Sioux, every tipi is the world in an image, the fire at the center represents *Wakan-Tanka* within the world. To emphasize the sacredness of this central fire, it should be recalled that, when the Sioux were still nomadic, a man was appointed to be the keeper of the fire, and he would usually have his tipi at the center of the camping circle. When camp was moved, this keeper would carry the fire in a small log, and when camp was set up again, each lodge would start its fire from this central source. The fire was extinguished and a new one started, always in a ritual manner, only after there had been some great catastrophe, or when a complete purification was needed for the whole camp.

23

"O *Wakan-Tanka,* behold the pipe! The smoke from this herb will cover everything upon earth, and will reach even to the heavens. May the way of Thy people be as this smoke. We have offered this pipe to You, and now I place within its bowl the sacred *kinnikinnik.* You have taught us that the round bowl of the pipe is the very center of the universe and the heart of man! O *Wakan-Tanka,* bend down to look upon us today; look upon Thy pipe with which we are about to send a voice, along with the winged peoples, the four-leggeds, and all the fruits of our Mother Earth. All that You have made will join with us in sending this voice!"

As he fills the pipe, the holy keeper makes the ritual offerings of tobacco to the six directions, with the following prayers: "O You, winged Power, there where the sun goes down, You are *wakan!* With You and through You we send a voice to *Wakan-Tanka* before releasing this soul. There is a place for You in this pipe. Help us! Give to our people Your red and blue days, that they may walk the sacred path of life in a *wakan* manner!

"O winged Power of the place where *Waziah* lives [the north]! purifier of the earth, of the two-leggeds, and of all that is unclean, with the soul of a two-legged person we are about to send a voice through You to *Wakan-Tanka.* There is a place for You in the pipe, and so help us in sending this voice! Give to us the two sacred days which You have!

"O You, winged One, of the place from whence the sun comes! You who are long-winged, and who controls knowledge, the Light of the universe, we are about to send a voice to *Wakan-Tanka* with this soul who has been with his people. You also have the two great red and blue days; give these to us, and help us in sending a voice!

"O You, sacred White Swan, of the place towards which we always face, You control the red path leading there where *Waziah* has his lodge. You guide all the four-legged and two-legged people who travel upon this sacred road. We are about to release a soul who is to travel upon Your path; through this soul we are sending a voice to *Wakan-Tanka!* Help us to send this voice, and give to us Your two sacred days!

"O You, Spotted Eagle, who are next to the heavens, close to *Wakan-Tanka!* Your wings are powerful. You are the one who takes care of our nation's sacred hoop and all that is within this circle. May all the people be happy and have many blessings! We are about to release a soul who will go on a long journey, in order that the steps of its generations to come will be *wakan.* There is a place for You in the pipe! Help us to send our voice to *Wakan-Tanka,* and give us the sacred red and blue days which are Yours!

"O *Wakan-Tanka,* we are about to offer to You this pipe. Look down upon us and upon our Grandmother and Mother Earth. Everything is *wakan* that is on our Mother, the earthly source of all life. The steps of our people are upon Her. May they be firm and strong! From You, Grandmother Earth, a soul is to be released. There is a place in this pipe for You, and for all Your sacred things and peoples! All together as one we send our voice to *Wakan-Tanka.* Help us to walk in a *wakan* manner pleasing to You! Give to us the sacred red and blue days which You control!"

In this manner, the whole universe was placed in the pipe, and then, turning to the people, the keeper of the pipe says: "Since we have done all this correctly, the soul should have a good journey, and it will help our people to increase and to walk the sacred path in a manner pleasing to *Wakan-Tanka.*"

And then to the soul he says: "O you soul, my grandchild, you are the root of this great rite; from you there will grow much that is *wakan.* Through this rite our people will learn to be generous, to help those in need, and to follow in every way the teachings of *Wakan-Tanka.* O soul, this is your day. The time has now come!

"There will be four virgins who will always carry with them the power of these rites. You, O soul, will cover them over with your sacred buffalo robe. This is your day; it is one of joy, for much Light has come to our people. All that has been with you in the past is here with you today. Your relatives have arrived with food, which will be purified, offered to you, and then given to the four virgins; after this it will be shared with the poor and unfortunate ones. But now the time has come for us to offer up this pipe

to *Wakan-Tanka,* and then to smoke it.[11] We offer to Him everything that is in the universe; we send our voices to Him through
this pipe. *Hetchetu welo!*

"*Hee-ay-hay-ee-ee!* [four times] *Tunkashila Wakan-Tanka,*
Grandfather, Great Spirit, look down upon us! This is the *wakan*
day for this soul. May he help the coming generations to walk in a
sacred manner! We are offering this pipe to You, O *Wakan-Tanka,*
and ask You to help this soul, his relatives, and all the people! Behold the pipe, and bend down to look upon us as we fulfill Thy
will! From this earth we are sending a voice to You! Be merciful
to us, and to this soul who will be released from the center of his
people's hoop! O Grandfather, *Wakan-Tanka,* be merciful to us,
that our people may live!"

To this all the people say: "*Hi yee!* Thanks! So be it!" and then
the keeper lights the pipe, smokes it for a few puffs, and hands it to
the keeper of the soul, who offers it to heaven, earth, and the four
directions. After smoking it a little, he passes it around sun-wise,
that all the people may smoke. As each man smokes, he asks some
blessing, and when the pipe comes back to the keeper of the pipe,
it is purified, and the ashes are carefully placed in a special buckskin bag.

After the pipe has been offered up to *Wakan-Tanka,* the keeper
begins to cry, and soon all the people are crying.

I should, perhaps, explain to you here, that it is good to cry at
this moment, for it shows that we are thinking of the soul and of
death, which must come to all created beings and things; and it
is also a sign that we are humiliating ourselves before the Great
Spirit, for we know that we are as dust before Him, who is everything, and who is all powerful.

[11] It should be noticed that in the complete ritual of the pipe, there are
three distinct phases: the *purification* with the smoke of a sacred herb; the
"expansion" of the pipe so that it includes the entire universe; and finally,
what could be called the "identity," which is the sacrifice of the whole universe in the fire.

These three phases of the rite are common, in one form or another, to
all traditional or orthodox methods of prayer, and they always constitute
the prerequisite stages for a true spiritual realization. See Frithjof Schuon,
L'Oeil du Coeur (Paris, 1950); especially the chapter "De la Meditation."

All the food that is to be given to the soul is placed outside the lodge; this food the women pick up and enter the lodge. Within the lodge, on the south side, a willow post will have been set up, as high as a man, and around the top of it a piece of buckskin is tied, upon which a face has been painted. On top of this face there is a war bonnet, and around the post there has been placed a buffalo robe. This figure represents the soul, and leaning against him are his bows and arrows, knives, and all his possessions. As the women enter with the food, they pass around the lodge sun-wise. Stopping at the south, they each hug the "soul post"; then, after leaving their food, they walk out of the lodge.

A small bit of each food that has been brought for the soul is put into a wooden bowl, and this is placed in front of the two holy men who are seated at the west. Four pure virgins then enter and take their places at the north of the lodge, for the Power of this direction is purity. The keeper of the pipe then stands and speaks to the soul.

"You, O soul, are the *hokshichankiya* [spiritual influence, or seed]! You are as the root of the *wakan* tree which is at the center of our nation's hoop. May this tree bloom! May our people and the winged and the four-legged peoples all flourish! O soul, your relatives have brought you this food which you will soon eat, and, by this act, goodness will spread among the people. O soul, *Wakan-Tanka* has given to you four relatives who are sitting there at the north; they represent our true relatives: Grandfather and Father, *Wakan-Tanka*, and Grandmother and Mother, *Maka,* the Earth. Remember these four relatives, who are all really One, and, with Them in mind, look back upon your people as you travel upon the great path!"

A small hole is dug at the foot of the "soul post," and the keeper of the pipe holds the wooden bowl, in which is the purified food, towards the hole, saying to the soul: "You are about to eat this *wakan* food. When it is placed in your mouth its influence will spread, and it will cause the fruits of our Mother, the Earth, to increase and prosper. Your Grandmother is *wakan;* upon Her we stand as we place this food in your mouth. Do not forget us when you go forth to *Wakan-Tanka,* but look back upon us!"

The food is placed in the hole, and on top of it the juice of the wild cherry is poured, for this juice is the water of Life. The hole is then covered over with dirt, for the soul has finished its last meal.

The four virgins then prepare to eat the sacred buffalo meat and to drink the cherry juice; but first the food is purified over the smoke of the sweet grass, and then the keeper of the pipe speaks to the virgins, saying: "Grandchildren, you are now to receive the *hokshichankiya* of the soul; this will cause you and your fruits to be always *wakan.* Grandchildren, remember to share your food—all you have—for in the world there are always the needy, orphans, and old people. But above all, my grandchildren, never forget your four great relatives, who are represented by your relatives here on earth! You are now to eat and drink the sacred fruit of Mother Earth, and through this you and your fruits will be *wakan.* Always remember this my children!"

The keeper of pipe picks up the bowl of food, and each time that he places food in the mouth of a virgin, he says: "I place this food in your mouth. It is sweet and fragrant—*wakan!* The people will see your generations to come!"

The four virgins stoop and drink the juice of the wild cherry which is in the wooden bowl on the ground, and when they have finished eating and drinking, the keeper says to them: "Grandchildren, all that we have done here today is *lela wakan,* for it has all been done according to the instructions given to us by the holy woman, who was also a buffalo, and who brought to us our most holy pipe. She told us that she had four ages; you, too, grandchildren, have these ages. Understand all this deeply, for it is important. It is a great thing we are doing here today. It is so indeed! *Hetchetu welo!"*

The keeper of the pipe then walks around to the south and, picking up the "soul bundle," says to it: "Grandchild, you are about to leave on a great journey. Your father and mother and all your relatives have loved you. Soon they will be happy."

The father of the child then embraces the sacred bundle, by

holding it to each shoulder, and after he has done this, the keeper says to him: "You loved your son, and you have kept him at the center of our people's hoop. As you have been good to this your loved one, so be good to all other people! The sacred influence of your son's soul will be upon the people; it is as a tree that will always bloom."

He then walks around to the north, and as he touches each virgin with the sacred bundle, he says: "The tree which was selected to be at the center of your sacred hoop is this! May it always flourish and bloom in a *wakan* manner!" Then, holding the bundle up towards the heavens, he cries: "Always look back upon your people, that they may walk the sacred path with firm steps!"

This, the keeper cries four times as he walked towards the door of the lodge, and, as he stops the fourth time just outside the door, he cries with a very shrill voice: "Behold your people! Look back upon them!"

The moment the bundle passes out of the lodge,[12] the soul is released; it has departed on the "spirit trail" leading to *Wakan-Tanka.*[13]

Once the soul has left the bundle containing the lock of hair,

---

[12] The significance of this ritual act will be clear if it is recalled that the tipi is the universe, the cosmos; and the space outside the tipi is symbolically the Infinite, or *Wakan-Tanka.*

It is in this same manner that the Plains Indians release the souls which they have taken in the scalps of the enemy.

"The chief . . . looks upward through the opening in the roof, into the blue sky above, then with a quick movement he thrusts the slender poles on which are suspended scalps, through the opening to the sky and pulls them in again, by which act the Spirits of the slain are released." (Francis La Flesche, "War and Peace Ceremony of the Osage Indians," *Bulletin No. 101 of the Bureau of American Ethnology.*)

[13] It is held by the Sioux that the released soul travels southward along the "Spirit Path" (the Milky Way) until it comes to a place where this way divides. Here an old woman, called *Maya owichapaha,* sits; "She who pushes them over the bank," who judges the souls; the worthy ones she allows to travel on the path which goes to the right, but the unworthy she "pushes over the bank," to the left. Those who go to the right attain union with *Wakan-Tanka,* but the ones who go to the left must remain in a conditioned state until they become sufficiently purified.

it is no longer especially *wakan,* but it may be kept by the family, if they wish, as something of a remembrance. The four holy virgins are each given a buffalo robe, and then they leave the lodge immediately after the keeper of the pipe.

With this, the rite is finished, and then the people all over the camp are happy and rejoice, and they rush up to touch the four virgins who are *lela wakan,* and who will always bear with them this great influence, bringing great strength to the people. Gifts are given out to the poor and unfortunate ones, and everywhere there is feasting and rejoicing. It is indeed a good day. *Hetchetu welo!*

CHAPTER III

Inipi: THE RITE OF PURIFICATION

The rite of the *onikare* (sweat lodge) utilizes all the Powers of the universe: earth, and the things which grow from the earth, water, fire, and air. The water represents the Thunder-beings who come fearfully but bring goodness, for the steam which comes from the rocks, within which is the fire, is frightening, but it purifies us so that we may live as *Wakan-Tanka* wills, and He may even send to us a vision if we become very pure.

When we use the water in the sweat lodge we should think of *Wakan-Tanka* who is always flowing, giving His power and life to everything; we should even be as water which is lower than all things, yet stronger even than the rocks.

The sweat lodge is made from twelve or sixteen young willows, and these, too, have a lesson to teach us, for in the fall their leaves die and return to the earth, but in the spring they come to

31

life again. So, too, men die but live again in the real world of *Wakan-Tanka*, where there is nothing but the spirits of all things; and this true life we may know here on earth if we purify our bodies and minds, thus coming closer to *Wakan-Tanka*, who is all-purity.

The willows which make the frame of the sweat lodge are set up in such a way that they mark the four quarters of the universe; thus, the whole lodge is the universe in an image, and the two-legged, four-legged, and winged peoples, and all things of the world are contained within it, for all these peoples and things too must be purified before they can send a voice to *Wakan-Tanka*.

The rocks which we use represent Grandmother Earth, from whom all fruits come, and they also represent the indestructible and everlasting nature of *Wakan-Tanka*. The fire which is used to heat the rocks represents the great power of *Wakan-Tanka* which gives life to all things; it is as a ray from the sun, for the sun is also *Wakan-Tanka* in a certain aspect.

The round fireplace at the center of the sweat lodge is the center of the universe, in which dwells *Wakan-Tanka*, with His power which is the fire. All these things are *wakan* to us and must be understood deeply if we really wish to purify ourselves, for the power of a thing or an act is in the meaning and the understanding.

The sweat lodge is always constructed with its door to the east, for it is from this direction that the light of wisdom comes. About ten paces from the lodge, at the east, we first construct a sacred fireplace which is called *Peta-owihankeshni*, "fire of no end," or "eternal fire," and this is where the rocks are heated. To make this sacred fireplace, we first place four sticks running east and west, and on top of these we place four sticks running north and south, and then around these we lean sticks as in a tipi, first on the west side, and then on the north, east, and south sides; rocks are then placed at these four directions, and then many more are piled on top. But as we build this fire, we should pray.

"O Grandfather, *Wakan-Tanka*, You are and always were. I am about to do Thy will on this earth as You have taught us. In

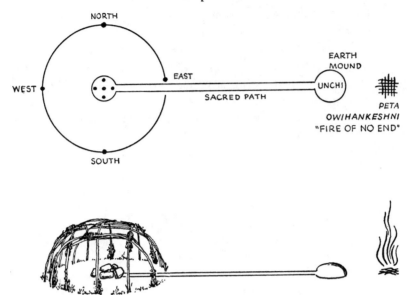

The *Inipi:* "Purification Lodge"

placing these sacred rocks at the four quarters, we understand that it is You who are at the center. O sacred rocks, you are helping us to do the will of *Wakan-Tanka!*"

And as we light the fire, always on the side facing the east, we pray: "O *Wakan-Tanka*, this is Your eternal fire that has been given to us on this great island! It is Your will that we build this place in a sacred manner. The eternal fire always burns; through it we shall live again by being made pure, and by coming closer to Your powers."

In making the central altar within the sweat lodge, where later the heated rocks will be placed, we first push a stick into the earth at the center of the lodge, and then around this point we draw a circle with a cord of rawhide. While fixing this holy center, we should pray.

"O Grandfather and Father *Wakan-Tanka*, maker of all that is, who always has been, behold me! And You, Grandmother and

33

Mother Earth, You are *wakan* and have holy ears; hear me! We have come from You, we are a part of You, and we know that our bodies will return to You at that time when our spirits travel upon the great path. By fixing this center in the earth, I remember You to whom my body will return, but above all I think of *Wakan-Tanka*, with whom our spirits become as one. By purifying myself in this way, I wish to make myself worthy of You, O *Wakan-Tanka*, that my people may live!"

A round hole is now made at the center of the sweat lodge, and with the dirt which is taken out a sacred path is made leading out of the lodge to the east, and at the end of this path a small mound is built; when doing this we pray.

"Upon You, Grandmother Earth, I shall build the sacred path of life. By purifying ourselves for the people, we shall walk this path with firm steps, for it is the path leading even to *Wakan-Tanka*. Upon this path there are four steps which are sacred. May my people walk this path! May we be pure! May we live again!"

And now, sending a voice directly to *Wakan-Tanka*, we cry: "Grandfather *Wakan-Tanka*, we have learned Thy will, and we know the sacred steps we are to take. With the help of all things and all beings we are about to send our voice to You. Be merciful to us! Help us! I place myself upon this sacred path, and send my voice to You through the four Powers, which we know are but one Power. Help me in all this! O my Grandfather *Wakan-Tanka*, be merciful to us! Help my people and all things to live in a sacred manner pleasing to You! Help us O *Wakan-Tanka* to live again!"

He who leads the purification rite, now enters the lodge alone and with his pipe. He passes around sun-wise and sits at the west and makes an altar of the central hole by placing pinches of tobacco at its four corners. A glowing coal is passed into the lodge and is placed at the center. The leader then burns sweet grass and rubs the smoke all over his body, feet, head, hands, and the pipe too is purified over the smoke; everything is made sacred, and if there is anything in the lodge that is not good it is driven away by the Power of the smoke.

The leader should now offer a pinch of tobacco to the winged

Power of the place where the sun goes down, from which the purifying waters come; this Power is invoked and is asked to help in the rite. After this the sacred tobacco is placed in the pipe, and in the same manner pinches of tobacco are offered to the Powers of the north, whence come the purifying winds; to the east, the place where the sun comes up, and from whence comes wisdom; to the south which is the source and end of all life; above to the heavens, and finally to Mother Earth. As the aid of each Power is invoked and as each pinch of tobacco is placed in the pipe, all those outside the lodge cry "How!" for they are glad and satisfied that this sacred thing has been done.

Now that the pipe has been filled, and everything made *wakan,* the leader leaves the lodge, walks to the east along the sacred path, and then places the pipe on the earth mound, with the bowl on the west side, and with the stem slanting to the east.

All who are to be purified now enter the lodge, the leader first, and as each bows low to enter, he prays.

"Hi ho! Hi ho! Pila miya [Thanks]! By bowing low in order to enter this lodge, I am remembering that I am as nothing compared with You, O *Wakan-Tanka,* who are everything. It is You who have placed us upon this island; we are the last to be created by You who are first and who always have been. Help me to become pure, before I send my voice to You! Help us in all that which we are about to do!"

Once within the lodge, the men move around sun-wise and then sit on the sacred sage which had been strewn upon the earth; the leader sits at the east, just beside the door. All remain silent a little while, remembering the goodness of *Wakan-Tanka,* and how it was He who made all things. Then the pipe is handed into the lodge by the helper, who is often a woman, and who remains outside during the rite. The man who sits at the west takes the pipe and places it in front of him, with its stem pointing towards the west.

With a forked stick, the helper now picks up one of the rocks from the sacred fire, *Peta owihankeshni,* and, walking along the sacred path, he hands the rock inside the lodge, where it is placed at the center of the round altar; this first rock is for *Wakan-Tan-ka,* who is always at the center of everything. The man seated at the west touches the foot of the pipe to the rock, and each time that a rock is placed on the altar he touches the pipe to it, and all the men cry: "Hi ye! *Pila miya!* [Thanks]!"

The second rock to be handed into the lodge is placed at the west of the altar, the next at the north, then one for the east, one for the south, one for earth, and finally the hole is filled up with the rest of the rocks, and all these together represent everything that there is in the universe.

The person at the west now offers the pipe to heaven, earth, and the four directions, and then he lights it, and after a few puffs (rubbing the smoke all over his body) he hands the pipe to the one at his left, saying: *"Ho Ate,"* or *"Ho Tunkashila,"* according to their relationship. The one who takes the pipe says in turn: *"How Ate"* or *"How Tunkashila,"* and in this manner the pipe is passed sun-wise around the circle. When the pipe comes back to the man at the west, he purifies it, lest some impure person may have touched it, and carefully empties the ashes, placing them at the edge of the sacred altar. This first use of the pipe within the lodge reminds us of the holy White Buffalo Cow Woman, who long ago entered our lodge in a sacred manner, and then left.

The pipe passes around to the leader sitting at the east, who holds it above the sacred altar, stem pointing to the west, and then moves it along the sacred path to the east, where the helper who is standing just outside the door takes it and, after filling it in a ritual manner, leans it against the sacred earth mound, with the bowl at the east, and the stem slanting towards the west, for the Power of the west is now to be invoked.

The helper closes the door of the sweat lodge, making it completely dark inside, and this darkness represents the darkness of the soul, our ignorance, from which we must now purify ourselves so that we may have the light. During the course of the *Inipi,* the door will be opened four times, letting in the light; this reminds us of the four ages, and how through the goodness of *Wakan-Tanka* we have received the Light in each of these ages.

The man at the west now sends a voice to *Wakan-Tanka* in this manner:

"Hee-ay-hay-ee-ee!" (four times)

(This we say whenever we are in need of help, or are in despair, and indeed are we not now in darkness and in need of the Light!)

"I am sending a voice!" (four times) "Hear me!" (Four times) *"Wakan-Tanka,* Grandfather, You are first and always have been. You have brought us to this great island, and here our people wish to live in a sacred manner. Teach us to know and to see all the powers of the universe, and give to us the knowledge to understand that they are all really one Power. May our people always send their voices to You as they walk the sacred path of life!

"O ancient rocks, *Tunkayatakapaka,* you are now here with us; *Wakan-Tanka* has made the Earth, and has placed you next to Her. Upon you the generations will walk, and their steps shall not falter! O Rocks, you have neither eyes, nor mouth, nor limbs; you do not move, but by receiving your sacred breath [the steam], our people will be long-winded as they walk the path of life; your breath is the very breath of life.

"There is a winged One, there where the sun goes down to rest, who controls those waters to which all living beings owe their lives. May we use these waters here in a sacred manner!

"O you people who are always standing, who pierce up through the earth, and who reach even unto the heavens, you tree-people are very many, but one of you has been especially chosen for supporting this sacred purification lodge. You trees are the protectors of the wingeds, for upon you they build their lodges and raise their families; and beneath you there are many people whom you shelter. May all these people and all their generations walk together as relatives!

"To every earthly thing, O *Wakan-Tanka,* You have given a power, and because the fire is the most powerful of Your creations, since it consumes all other things, we place it here at our center, and when we see it and think of it, we really remember

You. May this sacred fire always be at our center! Help us in that which we are about to do!"

The leader now sprinkles water on the rocks, once for our Grandfather, *Tunkashila,* once for our Father, *Ate,* once for our Grandmother, *Unchi,* once for our Mother, *Ina,* the Earth, and then once for the sacred pipe; this is done with a sprig of sage or sweet grass, so that the steam will be fragrant, and as it rises and fills the little lodge, the leader cries: "O *Wakan-Tanka,* behold me! I am the people. In offering myself to You, I offer all the people as one, that they may live! We wish to live again! Help us!"

It is now very hot in the lodge, but it is good to feel the purifying qualities of the fire, the air, and the water, and to smell the fragrance of the sacred sage. After these powers have worked well into us, the door of the lodge is thrown open, reminding us of the first age in which we received the Light from *Wakan-Tanka.* Water is now brought in, and the leader at the east passes it around sun-wise, and each man drinks a little, or rubs it over his body. As we do this we think of the place where the sun goes down, and from which comes the water, and the Power of this direction helps us to pray.

The helper outside the lodge then takes the filled pipe from the earth mound, offers it to Heaven and Earth, and walking along the sacred path, hands the pipe—stem first—to the person sitting at the west of the lodge. This man offers the pipe to the six directions, smokes it a little (rubbing the smoke all over his body) after which it is passed around the circle until it has been smoked up. The man at the west then empties the pipe, placing the burned tobacco beside the central altar, and hands the pipe out as before. The helper again fills the pipe, and leans it against the sacred mound, with the stem leaning to the north, for, during the second period of darkness within the lodge, the Power of the winged One of the north will be invoked.

The door of the lodge is closed, and we are in darkness for the second time. It is the person at the north who now prays.

"Behold, O you Baldheaded Eagle, there where the giant *Waziah* has his lodge! *Wakan-Tanka* has placed you there to control this Path; you are there to guard the health of the people, that they may live. Help us with your cleansing wind! May it make us pure so that we may walk the sacred path in a holy manner, pleasing to *Wakan-Tanka*.

"O Grandfather *Wakan-Tanka*, You are above everything! It is You who have placed a sacred rock upon the earth, which is now at the center of our hoop. You have given to us also the fire; and there at the place where the sun goes down, you have given power to *Wakinyan-Tanka* who controls the waters and who guards the most sacred pipe.[1] You have placed a winged One at the place where the sun comes up, who gives to us wisdom; and You have also placed a winged One at the place towards which we always face; He is the source of life, and He leads us on the sacred red path. All these powers, are Your power, and they are really one; they are all now here within this lodge."

[1] The great Thunderbird of the west: *Wakinyan-Tanka,* is one of the most important and profound aspects of Siouan religion. The Indian describes Him as living "in a lodge on the top of a mountain at the edge of the world where the sun goes down. He is many, but they are only as One; He is shapeless, but He has wings with four joints each; He has no feet, yet He has huge talons; He has no head, yet has a huge beak with rows of teeth in it like the teeth of the wolf; His voice is the thunder clap and rolling thunder is caused by the beating of His wings on the clouds; He has an eye, and its glance is lightning. In a great cedar tree beside His lodge He has His nest made of dry bones, and in it is an enormous egg from which His young continually issue. He devours His young and they each become one of His many selves. He flies through all the domain of the sky, hidden in a robe of clouds . . . . His functions are to cleanse the world from filth and to fight the Monsters who defile the Waters. His symbol is a zigzag red line forked at each end." (J. R. Walker, *The Sun Dance and other Ceremonies of the Oglala Division of the Teton Dakota* [Anthropological Papers of the American Museum of Natural History, XVI, Part II] [New York, 1917].)

This Thunderbird is really *Wakan-Tanka* as the giver of Revelation, (symbolized by the lightning); He is the same as the great one-eyed Bird, *Garuda,* of the Hindu tradition, or the Chinese Dragon (the Logos), who rides on the clouds of the storm, and whose voice is the thunder. As giver of Revelation he is identical in function to the Archangel Gabriel of Judaism or Christianity—the *Jibrail* of Islam.

It is fitting that the Thunderbird is for the Indian the protector of the sacred pipe, for the pipe, like the lightning, is the axis joining heaven and earth.

"O *Wakan-Tanka,* Grandfather, above all, it is Thy will that we are doing here. Through that Power which comes from the place where the giant *Waziah* lives, we are now making ourselves as pure and as white as new snow. We know that we are now in darkness, but soon the Light will come. When we leave this lodge may we leave behind all impure thoughts, all ignorance. May we be as children newly born! May we live again, O *Wakan-Tanka!"*

Water is now put on the rocks, four times for the Powers of the four directions, and as the steam rises we sing a song, or even just a chant, for this helps us to understand the mystery of all things.

The door of the lodge is soon opened for the second time, representing the coming of the purifying Power of the north, and also we see the light which destroys darkness, just as wisdom drives away ignorance. Water is passed to the leader at the east, who offers it to the men, mentioning his relationship to each, as I have described before.

The pipe is again handed into the lodge, and is given to the person sitting at the north; he offers it to the six directions, lights it, and after a few puffs (rubbing the smoke all over himself) he passes it around the circle. When all the *kinnikinnik* has been smoked up, the pipe is returned to the north, where it is purified, and the ashes are placed by the central altar. Then the pipe is handed out to the helper who again fills it and leans it upon the mound, this time with the stem pointing to the east, for we shall now invoke the Power of this direction. The door of the lodge is closed, and the man sitting at the east of the lodge now sends his voice in this manner:

"O Great Spirit, *Wakan-Tanka,* I have just seen the day, the Light of life. There where the sun comes up, You have given the power of wisdom to the Morning Star. The winged One who guards this path is long-winded, and with the two sacred days which You, O *Wakan-Tanka,* have given to Him, He has guarded the path of the people. O You who control that path where the sun comes up, look upon us with Your red and blue days, and help us in sending our voices to *Wakan-Tanka!* O You who have knowledge, give some of it to us, that our hearts may be enlightened, and that we may know all that is sacred!

"O Morning Star, there at the place where the sun comes up; O You who have the wisdom which we seek, help us in cleansing ourselves and all the people, that our generations to come will have Light as they walk the sacred Path. You lead the dawn as it walks forth, and also the day which follows with its Light which is knowledge; this You do for us and for all the people of the world, that they may see clearly in walking the *wakan* path; that they may know all that is holy, and that they may increase in a sacred manner!"

Water is again poured on the rocks and we begin to sing a sacred chant. In a short time, when the heat has worked all through us, the door is opened for the third time, and the light of the east comes in upon us. As the pipe is handed in to the man at the east, all the men cry: *"Hi ho! Hi ho!* [Thanks!]" and the leader holds the pipe up to heaven and sends his voice:

"Wakan-Tanka, we give thanks for the Light which You have given to us through the Power of the place where the sun comes up. Help us, O You Power of the east! Be merciful to us!"

The pipe is then lit and smoked around the circle, and again when we have finished, the helper takes it and this time leans it against the mound with its stem slanting to the south. Water is again passed around sun-wise, and is rubbed all over the body, especially on top of the head, and then the door is closed for the last time. It is the man at the south who now sends his voice.

"Grandfather, *Wakan-Tanka,* behold us! You have placed a great Power there where we always face, and from this direction many generations have come forth, and have returned. There is a winged One at this direction who guards the sacred red path, from which the generations have come forth. The generation which is here today wishes to cleanse and purify itself, that it may live again!

"We shall burn the sweet grass as an offering to *Wakan-Tanka,* and the fragrance of this will spread throughout heaven and earth; it will make the four-leggeds, the wingeds, the star peoples of the heavens, and all things as relatives. From You, O Grandmother earth, who are lowly, and who support us as does a mother, this fragrance will go forth; may its power be felt throughout the universe, and may it purify the feet and hands of the two-leggeds, that they may walk forward upon the sacred earth, raising their heads to *Wakan-Tanka!*"

All that is left of the water is now poured upon the rocks, which are still very hot, and as the steam rises and penetrates everything, we sing or chant a sacred song. Soon the leader of the *Inipi* says: "The helper will soon open the door for the last time, and when it is open we shall see the Light. For it is the wish of *Wakan-Tanka* that the Light enters into the darkness, that we may see not only with our two eyes, but with the one eye which is of the heart [*Chante Ishta*], and with which we see and know all that is true and good.[2] We give thanks to the helper; may his generations be blessed! It is good! It is finished! *Hetchetu alo!*"

As the door of the lodge is opened, all the men cry: *"Hi ho! Hi ho!* Thanks!," and the men are all happy, for they have come forth from the darkness and are now living in the Light.[3] The helper then brings a live coal from the sacred fire, and places it just outside the doorway of the lodge, upon the sacred path. As he burns the sweet grass upon the coal, he says: "This is the fragrance of *Wakan-Tanka.* Through this the two-leggeds, the four-leggeds, the winged ones, and all the peoples of the universe, will be happy, and will rejoice!"

The leader of the rite then says: "This is the fire that will help the generations to come, if they use it in a sacred manner. But if they do not use it well, the fire will have the power to do them great harm."

[2] For a commentary on the "Eye of the Heart," see Frithjof Schuon, *L'Oeil du Coeur.*

[3] Entering into the light after being in the darkness of the purification lodge represents liberation from the universe, the cosmos, or microcosmically the liberation from the ego; both ego and world are "dark" since they have only a relative or illusory reality, for ultimately there is no reality other than *Wakan-Tanka,* who is here represented by the light of day, or by the space around the lodge.

This liberation from the cosmos, or from the individuality, is especially well represented in the purification rite of the Osage Indians: "At the close

The leader purifies his hands and feet over the smoke, and, raising his hands to heaven, he prays: *"Hi ho! Hi ho!"* (four times) *"Wakan-Tanka,* today You have been good to us; for this we give thanks. I now place my feet upon the Earth. With great happiness I walk upon the sacred Earth, our Mother. May the generations to come also walk in this sacred manner!"

Moving around sun-wise, all the men now leave the sweat lodge, and they too purify their hands and feet, and pray to *Wakan-Tanka* as their leader had done.

This most sacred rite has now been finished, and those who have participated are as men born again, and have done much good not only for themselves, but for the whole nation.

I should perhaps mention, that, often, when we are inside the sweat lodge, little children poke their heads inside, and ask the Great Spirit to make their lives pure. We do not chase them away, for we know that little children already have pure hearts.

When we leave the sweat lodge we are as the souls which are kept, as I have described, and which return to *Wakan-Tanka* after they have been purified; for we, too, leave behind in the *Inipi* lodge all that is impure, that we may live as the Great Spirit wishes, and that we may know something of that real world of the Spirit, which is behind this one.

These rites of the *Inipi* are very *wakan* and are used before any great undertaking for which we wish to make ourselves pure or for which we wish to gain strength; and in many winters past our men, and often the women, made the *Inipi* even every day, and sometimes several times in a day, and from this we received much of our power. Now that we have neglected these rites we have lost much of this power; it is not good, and I cry when I think of it. I pray often that the Great Spirit will show to our young people the importance of these rites.

of the ceremony the Chief . . . tells the men that each one must grasp one of the frame poles of the little house, and when they have done so he calls out: 'There is no other way out, my valiant men!' and all the men acting in concert, toss the little house upward, towards the setting sun." (Francis La Flesche, "War and Peace Ceremony of the Osage Indians," *Bulletin No. 101 of the Bureau of American Ethnology.*)

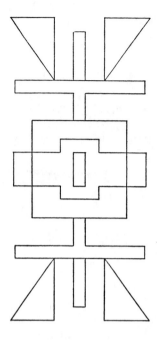

CHAPTER IV

Hanblecheyapi: CRYING FOR A VISION

The "Crying for a Vision" ritual, like the purification rites of the *Inipi,* was used long before the coming of our most sacred pipe. This way of praying is very important, and indeed it is at the center of our religion, for from it we have received many good things, even the four great rites which I shall soon describe.

Every man can cry for a vision, or "lament"; and in the old days we all—men and women—"lamented" all the time. What is received through the "lamenting" is determined in part by the character of the person who does this, for it is only those people who are very qualified who receive the great visions, which are interpreted by our holy man, and which give strength and health to our nation. It is very important for a person who wishes to "lament" to receive aid and advice from a *wichasha wakan* (holy man),[1] so that everything is done correctly, for if things are not done in the right way, something very bad can happen, and even a serpent could come and wrap itself around the "lamenter."

You have all heard of our great chief and priest Crazy Horse, but perhaps you did not know that he received most of his great power through the "lamenting" which he did many times a year, and even in the winter when it is very cold and very difficult. He received visions of the Rock, the Shadow, the Badger, a prancing horse (from which he received his name), the Day, and also of *Wanbli Galeshka,* the Spotted Eagle, and from each of these he received much power and holiness.[2]

There are many reasons for going to a lonely mountaintop to "lament." Some young men receive a vision when they are very young and when they do not expect it,[3] and then they go to "la-

---

[1] Throughout this work I have translated *wichasha wakan* as "holy man" or "priest," rather than "Medicine man," which has been used incorrectly in many books on the Indians. The Lakota term for "medicine man" or "doctor" is really *pejuta wichasa.* In order to clarify these frequently confused terms, I cannot do better than to quote the explanation given by Sword, an Oglala Sioux, to J. R. Walker: *"Wicasa wakan* is the term for a Lakota priest of the old religion; a Lakota medicine man is called *pejuta wacasa.* The white people call our *wicasa wakan,* medicine man, which is a mistake. Again, they say a *wicasa wakan* is making medicine when he is performing ceremonies. This is also a mistake. The Lakota call a thing "medicine" only when it is used to cure the sick or wounded, the proper term (for medicine) being *pejuta."* (*The Sun Dance . . . of the Teton Dakota* [Anthropological Papers of the American Museum of Natural History, XVI, Part II, 152].)

[2] The Indian actually identifies himself with, or becomes, the quality or principle of the being or thing which comes to him in a vision, whether it be a beast, a bird, one of the elements, or really any aspect of creation. In order that this "power" may never leave him, he always carries with him some material form representing the animal or object from which he has received his "power." These objects have often been incorrectly called fetishes, whereas they actually correspond more precisely to what the Christian calls guardian angels, since for the Indian, the animals and birds, and all things, are the "reflections"—in a material form—of the Divine principles. The Indian is only attached to the form for the sake of the principle which is contained within the form.

[3] Black Elk himself received his great vision when he was only nine years old. For a description of this vision, see Neihardt's *Black Elk Speaks,* chap. III.

45

ment" that they might understand it better. Then we "lament" if we wish to make ourselves brave for a great ordeal such as the Sun Dance or to prepare for going on the warpath. Some people "lament" in order to ask some favor of the Great Spirit, such as curing a sick relative; and then we also "lament" as an act of thanksgiving for some great gift which the Great Spirit may have given to us. But perhaps the most important reason for "lamenting" is that it helps us to realize our oneness with all things, to know that all things are our relatives; and then in behalf of all things we pray to *Wakan-Tanka* that He may give to us knowledge of Him who is the source of all things, yet greater than all things.

Our women also "lament," after first purifying themselves in the *Inipi;* they are helped by other women, but they do not go up on a very high and lonely mountain. They go up on a hill in a valley, for they are women and need protection.

When a person wishes to "lament," he goes with a filled pipe to a holy man; he enters the tipi with the stem of the pipe pointing in front of him, and sits before the old man who is to be his guide. The "lamenter" then places the pipe on the ground with its stem now pointing towards himself, for it is he who wishes to gain knowledge. The holy man raises his hands above to *Wakan-Tanka* and to the four directions, and, taking up the pipe, he asks the man what he wishes.

"I wish to 'lament' and offer my pipe to *Wakan-Tanka.* I need your help and guidance, and wish you to send a voice for me to the Powers above."

To this the old man says: *"How!"* (It is good); and then they leave the tipi, and, walking a short distance, they face the west, the young man standing to the left of the holy man, and they are joined by any others who may happen to be present. All raise their right hands, and the old man prays, holding the stem of the pipe to the heavens.

"Hee-ay-hay-ee-ee! [four times.] Grandfather, *Wakan-Tanka,* You are first and always have been! Everything belongs to You. It is You who have created all things! You are One and alone, and

to You we are sending a voice. This young man here is in difficulty, and wishes to offer the pipe to You. We ask that You give help to him! Within a few days he will offer his body to You. Upon the sacred Earth, our Mother and Grandmother, he will place his feet in a sacred manner.

"All the Powers of the world, the heavens and the star peoples, and the red and blue sacred days; all things that move in the universe, in the rivers, the brooks, the springs, all waters, all trees that stand, all the grasses of our Grandmother, all the sacred peoples of the universe: Listen! A sacred relationship with you all will be asked by this young man, that his generations to come will increase and live in a holy manner.

"O You, winged One, there where the sun goes down, who guards our sacred pipe, help us! Help us to offer this pipe to *Wakan-Tanka,* that He may give a blessing to this young man!"

To this all the people cry *"How!"* and then they sit in a circle upon the ground. The old man offers the pipe to the six directions, lights it, and passes it first to the young man who is to "lament." The "lamenter" offers it up with a prayer, and then it is smoked by everybody in the circle. When the pipe is smoked out, it is handed back to the holy man, who cleans and purifies it and hands it back to the young man, asking him when he wishes to "lament," and a day is then decided upon.

When this chosen day arrives, the young man wears only his buffalo robe, breech cloth, and moccasins, and he goes with his pipe to the tipi of the holy man. Crying as he walks, he enters the lodge and places his right hand on the head of the old man, saying: *"Unshe ma la ye!"* (Be merciful to me!) He then lays the pipe in front of the holy man and asks for his help.

The old man replies: "We all know that the pipe is sacred, and with it you have now come crying. I shall help you, but you must always remember what I am going to tell you; in the winters to come you must walk with the instructions and advice which I give to you. You may "lament" from one to four days, or even longer if you wish; how many days do you choose?"

"I choose two days."

"Good! This, then, is what you must do: First you should build an *Inipi* lodge in which we shall purify ourselves, and for this you must select twelve or sixteen small willows. But before you cut the willows remember to take to them a tobacco offering; and as you stand before them you should say: 'There are many kinds of trees, but it is you whom I have chosen to help me. I shall take you, but in your place there will be others!' Then you should bring these trees back to where we shall make the lodge.

"In a sacred manner you must also gather the rocks and sage, and then you must make a bundle of five long sticks and also five bundles of twelve small sticks, all of which will be used as offerings. These sticks you should lean against the west side of the sweat lodge until we are ready to purify them. We shall also need the Ree twist tobacco, *kinnikinnik,* a tobacco cutting board, buckskin for the tobacco-offering bags, sweet grass, a bag of sacred earth, a knife, and a stone hatchet. These things you must secure yourself, and when you are ready we shall purify ourselves. *Hetchetu welo!"*

When the purification lodge has been built, and all the equipment gathered, the holy man enters the lodge and sits at the west; the "lamenter" enters next and sits at the north, and then a helper enters and sits just to the south of the holy man. A cold rock is brought into the lodge and is placed on the north side of the central altar, where it is purified with a short prayer by the holy man; it is then taken outside by a helper. This is the first rock to be placed on the fire (*peta owihankeshni*) which has been built to the east of the lodge.

Just east of the central altar, within the purification lodge, the helper scrapes a sacred place upon the earth, and upon this he places a hot coal. The holy man now moves around to the east, and, bending over the coal, he holds up a bit of sweet grass and prays in this manner:

"O Grandfather, *Wakan-Tanka,* behold us! Upon the sacred earth I place this Your herb. The smoke that rises from the earth and fire will belong to all that moves in the universe: the four-leggeds, the wingeds, and everything that moves and everything that is. This offering of theirs will now be given to You, O *Wakan-Tanka!* We shall make sacred all that we touch!"

As the sweet grass is put upon the coal, the other two men in the lodge cry, *"Hi ye!"* (Thanks), and as the smoke rises, the holy man rubs his hands in it and then rubs them over his body. In the same manner the "lamenter" and the helper purify themselves with the sacred smoke. The little bag of earth is also purified, and then the three men again take their places at the west, every movement being made, of course, in a sun-wise manner. The purified earth is now very carefully spread all around inside the sacred central hole, and this is done slowly and reverently for this earth represents the whole universe. The helper hands a stick to the holy man, who uses it to mark four places around the hole, the first at the west, and then at the north, east, and south. Next a cross is made by drawing a line on the ground from west to east, then one from the north to the south. All this is very sacred, for it establishes the four great Powers of the universe, and also the center which is the dwelling place of *Wakan-Tanka.* A helper now enters from the outside carrying a hot coal in a split stick; he walks slowly, stopping four times, and the last time the coal is placed upon the center of the cross.

Holding a pinch of sweet grass over the coal, the holy man prays: "My Grandfather, *Wakan-Tanka,* You are everything. And my Father, *Wakan-Tanka,* all things belong to You! I am about to place Your herb on this fire. Its fragrance belongs to You."

The old man then slowly lowers the sweet grass to the fire. The helper now takes up the pipe, and moving with it in a sun-wise direction, hands it to the holy man who prays with it in these words: "O *Wakan-Tanka,* behold Your pipe! I hold it over the smoke of this herb. O *Wakan-Tanka,* behold also this sacred place which we have made. We know that its center is Your dwelling place. Upon this circle the generations will walk. The four-leggeds, the two-leggeds, the wingeds, and the four Powers of the universe, all will behold this, Your place."

The holy man holds the pipe over the smoke, pointing the stem first to the west, and then to the north, the east, the south, and to

49

heaven, then he touches the earth with its foot. He purifies all the sacred equipment: the buffalo robe and all the offering sticks; and then he makes little bags of tobacco which he ties on the ends of the offering sticks.

The old holy man, now seated at the west, takes the tobacco cutting board and begins to chop and mix the *kinnikinnik*. He first judges carefully the size of the pipe, for he must make just enough to fill the pipe bowl and no more. Each time that he shaves off a little piece of the tobacco, he offers it to one of the quarters of the world, taking great care that no piece jumps off the board, for this would make the Thunder-beings very angry. When the mixing has been finished, the old man takes up the pipe with his left hand, and holding up a pinch of the *kinnikinnik* with his right hand, he prays.

"O *Wakan-Tanka,* my Father and Grandfather, You are first, and always have been! Behold this young man here who has a troubled mind. He wishes to travel upon the sacred path; he will offer this pipe to You. Be merciful to him and help him! The four Powers and the whole universe will be placed in the bowl of the pipe, and then this young man will offer it to You, with the help of the wingeds and all things.

"The first to be placed in the pipe is You, O winged Power of the place where the sun goes down. You with Your guards are ancient and sacred. Behold! There is a place for You in the pipe; help us with Your two sacred blue and red days!"

The holy man places this tobacco in the pipe, and then he holds up another pinch towards the place in the north where *Waziah* the Giant lives.

"O You, winged Power, there where the Giant has His lodge, from whence come the strong purifying winds: there is a place for you in the pipe; help us with the two sacred days which you have!"

The Power of this direction is placed in the pipe, and a third pinch of tobacco is held towards the east.

"O You where the sun comes up, who guard the light and who give knowledge, this pipe will be offered to *Wakan-Tanka!* There is a place here for you too; help us with Your sacred days!"

In the same manner the Power of the east is placed in the pipe; and now a pinch of tobacco is held towards the south, the place towards which we always face.

"O You who control the sacred winds, and who live there where we always face, Your breath gives life; and it is from You and to You that our generations come and go. This pipe is about to be offered to *Wakan-Tanka;* there is a place in it for You. Help us with the two sacred days which You have!"

In this manner all the Powers of the four directions have been placed within the bowl of the pipe, and now a pinch of the sacred tobacco is held up towards the heavens, and this is for *Wanbli Galeshka,* the Spotted Eagle, who is higher than all other created beings, and who represents *Wakan-Tanka:*

"O *Wanbli Galeshka,* who circles in the highest heavens, You see all things in the heavens and upon the earth. This young man is about to offer his pipe to *Wakan-Tanka,* in order that he may gain knowledge. Help him, and all those who send their voices to *Wakan-Tanka* through you. There is a place for You in the pipe; give to us Your two sacred red and blue days."

With this prayer the Spotted Eagle is placed in the bowl of the pipe, and now a pinch of the tobacco is held towards Earth, and the old man continues to pray:

"O *Unchi* and *Ina,* our Grandmother and Mother, You are sacred! We know that it is from You that our bodies have come. This young man wishes to become one with all things; he wishes to gain knowledge. For the good of all your peoples, help him! There is a place for you in the pipe; give to us your two sacred red and blue days!"

Thus the Earth, which is now in the tobacco, is placed in the pipe, and in this manner all the six Powers of the universe have here become one. But in order to make sure that all the peoples of the world are included in the pipe, the holy man offers small grains of tobacco for each of the following winged peoples: "O sacred King Bird, who flies on the two sacred days; You who raise families so well, may we increase and live in the same manner. This pipe will soon be offered to *Wakan-Tanka!* There is a place here

51

for You. Help us!" With the same prayer, small grains of tobacco are offered and placed in the pipe, for the meadow lark, the blackbird, the woodpecker, the snowbird, the crow, the magpie, the dove, the hawk, the eagle hawk, the bald eagle, and finally what is left of the tobacco is offered for the two-legged who is about to "lament," offering himself up to *Wakan-Tanka*.

The pipe is then sealed with tallow, for the "lamenter" will take it with him when he goes to the top of the mountain, and there he will offer it to *Wakan-Tanka;* but it will not be smoked until he finishes the "lamenting" and returns to the holy man.

All the offering poles and the equipment which have been purified, are now taken and are placed outside the lodge at the west. The three men leave the lodge and prepare for the *Inipi* by taking off all their clothes except the breech cloth. Any other men who may now be present are permitted to take part in this purification rite.

The "lamenter" enters the *Inipi* first and, moving around sunwise, sits at the west of the lodge. He takes up his pipe which had been left in the lodge (with its stem pointing to the east) and, turning it around sun-wise, holds it up in front of him; and he remains in this position for the first part of the rite. The holy man enters next and, passing behind the "lamenter," sits at the east, just beside the door. Any other men who wish to take part in the rite then fill in the remaining places; two men remain outside to act as helpers.

One of the helpers fills a pipe in a ritual manner, and this is handed in to the man who sits just at the left of the "lamenter." The rock which had previously been purified is also handed in— on a forked stick, for it is now very hot—and is placed at the center of the sacred hole. A second rock is then placed at the west in the sacred place, and the others are placed at the north, east, and south. As the rocks are put in place, the person who holds the pipe to be smoked in the rite touches its foot to each rock, and as he does this all the men cry: *"Hi ye! Hi ye!"* The pipe is then lit, offered to Heaven, Earth, and the four directions, and is smoked around the circle. As it passes around, each man mentions his relationship to the person next to him, and after everybody has smoked they all say together: *"mitakuye oyasin!"* (We are all relatives!). The one who lit the pipe now empties it, placing the ashes upon the center altar, and after purifying it he hands it to the left, and it is passed out of the lodge. The helper again fills the pipe and leans it on the sacred mound with the stem pointing to the west. The door of the lodge is closed, and the holy man at the east begins to pray in the darkness: "Behold! All that moves in the universe is here!" This is repeated by everybody in the lodge, and at the end they all say: *"How!"*

"Hee-ay-hay-ee-ee! [four times] I am sending a voice! Hear me! [four times] *Wakan-Tanka,* Grandfather, behold us! O *Wakan-Tanka,* Father, behold us! On this great island there is a two-legged who says that he will offer a pipe to You. On this day his promise will be fulfilled. To whom could one send a voice except to You, *Wakan-Tanka,* our Grandfather and Father. O *Wakan-Tanka,* this young man asks You to be merciful to him. He says that his mind is troubled and that he needs Your help. In offering this pipe to You, he will offer his whole mind and body. The time has now come; he will soon go to a high place, and there he will cry for Your aid. Be merciful to him!

"O You four Powers of the universe, you wingeds of the air, and all the peoples who move in the universe—you have all been placed in the pipe. Help this young man with the knowledge which has been given to all of you by *Wakan-Tanka.* Be merciful to him! O *Wakan-Tanka,* grant that this young man may have relatives; that he may be one with the four winds, the four Powers of the world, and with the light of the dawn. May he understand his relationship with all the winged peoples of the air. He will place his feet upon the sacred earth of a mountaintop; may he receive understanding there; may his generations to come be holy! All things give thanks to You, O *Wakan-Tanka,* who are merciful, and who help us all. We ask all this of You because we know that You are the only One, and that You have power over all things!"

As a little water is poured on the red hot rocks, all the men sing:

> *Grandfather, I am sending a voice!*
> *To the Heavens of the universe, I am sending a voice;*
> *That my people may live!*

As the men sing this, and as the hot steam rises, the "lamenter" cries, for he is humbling himself, remembering his nothingness in the presence of the Great Spirit.[4]

After a short time the door of the lodge is opened by the helper, and the "lamenter" now embraces his pipe, holding it first to one shoulder and then to the other, and crying all the time to the Great Spirit: "Be merciful to me! Help me!" This pipe is then passed around the circle, and all the other men embrace it and cry in the same manner. It is then passed out of the lodge to the helpers, who also embrace it and then lean it on the little mound, with its stem to the east; for this direction is the source of light and understanding.

The second pipe which is being used for the purification rite, and which had been leaning on the sacred mound with its stem to the west, is now handed into the lodge, and is given to the person sitting just to the left of the "lamenter." This pipe is lit, and after it has been smoked by everybody in the circle, it is passed out of the lodge. After this, water is passed around, and the "lamenter" is now allowed to drink all that he wishes, but he must be careful not to spill any or to put any on his body, for this would anger the Thunder-beings who guard the sacred waters, and then they might visit him every night that he "laments." The holy man tells the "lamenter" to rub his body with the sage, and then the door is closed once more. A prayer is said by the next holiest man in the lodge, one who has had a vision.

"On this sacred earth, the Thunder-beings have been merci-

---

[4] This humiliation in which the Indian makes himself "lower than even the smallest ant," as Black Elk once expressed it, is the same attitude as that which, in Christianity, is called the "spiritual poverty"; this poverty is the *faqr* of the Islamic tradition or the *balya* of Hinduism and is the condition of those who realize that in relation to the Divine principle their own individuality is as nothing.

ful to me, and have given to me a power from where the Giant *Waziah* lives. It was an eagle who came to me. He will see you too when you go to cry for a vision. Then from the place where the sun comes up, they sent to me a Baldheaded Eagle; he too will see you. From the place towards which we always face, they sent to me a winged one. They were very merciful to me. In the depths of the heavens there is a winged being who is next to *Wakan-Tanka;* He is the Spotted Eagle, and He too will behold you. You will be seen by all the Powers and by the sacred earth upon which you stand. They have given to me a good road to follow upon this earth; may you too know this way! Set your mind upon the meanings of these things, and you will see! All this is so; do not forget! *Hechetu welo!"*

This old man then sings:

> *They are sending a voice to me.*
> *From the place where the sun goes down,*
> *Our Grandfather is sending a voice to me.*
> *From where the sun goes down,*
> *They are talking to me as they come.*
> *Our Grandfather's voice is calling to me.*
> *That winged One there where the Giant lives,*
> *Is sending a voice to me. He is calling me.*
> *Our Grandfather is calling me!"*

As the old man chants this song, water is put on the rocks, and after the men have been in the hot fragrant steam and darkness for a short time, the door is opened, and the fresh air and light fill the little lodge. Once again the pipe is taken from the sacred mound and is handed in to the man at the north of the lodge. After it has been smoked it is placed again on the mound with its stem pointing to the east. The door is closed, and this time it is the holy man at the east who prays.

"O *Wakan-Tanka,* behold all that we do and ask here! O You, Power, there where the sun goes down, who control the waters: with the breath of your waters this young man is purifying himself. And you too, O very aged rocks who are helping us here, listen! You are firmly fixed upon this earth; we know that the winds cannot shake you. This young man is about to send his voice, crying for a vision. You are helping us by giving to him some of your power; through your breath he is being made pure.

"O eternal fire there where the sun comes up, from you this young man is gaining strength and light. O you standing trees, *Wakan-Tanka* has given you the power to stand upright. May this young man always have you as an example; may he hold firmly to you! It is good. *Hechetu welo!*"

All the men now chant again, and after a little while the door is opened, and the pipe is sent to the holy man at the east, who lights it, and after smoking for a few puffs, hands it around the circle. When the tobacco has been smoked up, the helper again takes the pipe and places it on the earth mound, with the stem leaning to the south. The door of the *Inipi* is closed for the last time, and now the holy man addresses his prayer to the rocks.

"O you ancient rocks who are sacred, you have neither ears nor eyes, yet you hear and see all things. Through your powers this young man has become pure, that he may be worthy to go to receive some message from *Wakan-Tanka*. The men who guard the door of this sacred lodge will soon open it for the fourth time, and we shall see the light of the world. Be merciful to the men who guard the door! May their generations be blessed!"

Water is placed on the rocks, which are still very hot, and after the steam has penetrated throughout the lodge for a short time, the door is opened, and all the men cry: *"Hi ho! Hi ho!* Thanks!"

The "lamenter" leaves the lodge first, and goes and sits upon the sacred path, facing the little mound, and crying all the while. One of the helpers then takes up the buffalo robe, which had been purified, and places it over the shoulders of the "lamenter"; and another helper takes the pipe which has been leaning all this time on the mound, and hands it to the "lamenter," who is now ready to go up to the high mountain, there to cry for a vision.

Three horses are brought, and upon two of these the bundles of offering sticks and some sacred sage are loaded; the "lamenter" rides on the third horse, and all this time he is crying most pitifully and is holding his pipe in front of him. When they arrive at the foot of the chosen mountain, the two helpers go on ahead with all the equipment in order to prepare the sacred place on the mountaintop. When they arrive they enter the chosen place by walking in a direction always away from their camping circle, and they go directly to the spot which they have chosen to be the center and place all the equipment here. At this center they first make a hole, in which they place some *kinnikinnik,* and then in this hole they set up a long pole with the offerings tied at the top. One of the helpers now goes about ten stride to the west, and in the same manner he sets up a pole here, tying offerings to it. He then goes to the center where he picks up another pole, and this he fixes at the north again returning to the center. In the same manner he sets up poles at the east and at the south. All this time the other helper has been making a bed of sage at the center, so that when the "lamenter" is tired he may lie with his head against the center pole, and his feet stretching towards the east. When everything has been finished the helpers leave the sacred place by the north path, and then return to the "lamenter" at the foot of the mountain.

The "lamenter" now takes off his moccasins and even his breech cloth—for if we really wish to "lament" we must be poor in the things of this world—and he walks alone up to the top of the mountain, holding his pipe in front of him, and carrying his buffalo robe which he will use at night. As he walks he cries continually: *"Wakan-Tanka onshimala ye oyate wani wachin cha!"* (O Great Spirit, be merciful to me that my people may live!)

Entering the sacred place, the "lamenter" goes directly to the center pole, where he faces the west, and holding up his pipe with both hands he continues to cry: "O *Wakan-Tanka,* have pity on me, that my people may live!" Then walking very slowly he goes to the pole at the west, where he offers up the same prayer, and then returns to the center. In the same manner he goes to the poles at the north, east, and south, always returning to the center each time. After completing one of these rounds, he raises his pipe to the heavens asking the wingeds and all things to help him, and then pointing the pipe stem to the Earth, he asks aid from all that grows upon our Mother.

All this takes very little time to tell, yet the "lamenter" should do it all so slowly and in such a sacred manner that often he may take an hour or even two to make one of these rounds. The "lamenter" can move in no other manner than this, which is in the form of a cross, although he may linger at any one place as long as he wishes; but all day long this is what he does, praying constantly, either out loud or silently to himself, for the Great Spirit is everywhere; he hears whatever is in our minds and hearts, and it is not necessary to speak to Him in a loud voice. The "lamenter" need not always use this prayer that I have given, for he may remain silent with his whole attention directed to the Great Spirit or to one of His Powers. He must always be careful lest distracting thoughts come to him, yet he must be alert to recognize any messenger which the Great Spirit may send to him, for these people often come in the form of an animal, even one as small and as seemingly insignificant as a little ant. Perhaps a Spotted Eagle may come to him from the west, or a Black Eagle from the north, or the Bald Eagle from the east, or even the Red-headed Woodpecker may come to him from the south. And even though none of these may speak to him at first, they are important and should be observed. The "lamenter" should also notice if one of the little birds should come, or even perhaps a squirrel. At first the animals or winged peoples may be wild, but soon they become tame, and the birds will sit on the poles, or even little ants or worms may crawl on the pipe. All these people are important, for in their own way they are wise and they can teach us two-leggeds much if we make ourselves humble before them. The most important of all the creatures are the wingeds, for they are nearest to the heavens, and are not bound to the earth as are the four-leggeds, or the little crawling people.

It may be good to mention here that it is not without reason that we humans are two-legged along with the wingeds; for you see the birds leave the earth with their wings, and we humans may also leave this world, not with wings, but in the spirit. This will help you to understand in part how it is that we regard all created beings as sacred and important, for everything has a *wochangi* or influence which can be given to us, through which we may gain a little more understanding if we are attentive.

All day long the "lamenter" sends his voice to *Wakan-Tanka* for aid, and he walks as we have described upon the sacred paths which form a cross. This form has much power in it, for whenever we return to the center, we know that it is as if we are returning to *Wakan-Tanka,* who is the center of everything; and although we may think that we are going away from Him, sooner or later we and all things must return to Him.

In the evening the "lamenter" is very tired, for you should remember that he may neither eat nor drink during the days that he cries for a vision. He may sleep on the bed of sage which had been prepared for him, and must lean his head against the center pole, for even though he sleeps he is close to *Wakan-Tanka,* and it is very often during sleep that the most powerful visions come to us; they are not merely dreams, for they are much more real and powerful and do not come from ourselves, but from *Wakan-Tanka.* It may be that we shall receive no vision or message from the Great Spirit the first time that we "lament," yet we may try many times, for we should remember that *Wakan-Tanka* is always anxious to aid those who seek Him with a pure heart. But of course much depends on the nature of the person who cries for a vision, and upon the degree to which he has purified and prepared himself.

In the evenings the Thunder-beings may come, and although they are very terrifying, they bring much good, and they test our strength and endurance. Then too they help us to realize how really very small and insignificant we are compared to the great powers of *Wakan-Tanka.*

I remember one time when I "lamented," and a great storm came from the place where the sun goes down, and I talked with the Thunder-beings who came with hail and thunder and lightning and much rain, and the next morning I saw that there was

59

hail all piled up on the ground around the sacred place, yet inside it was perfectly dry. I think that they were trying to test me. And then, on one of the nights the bad spirits came and started tearing the offerings off the poles; and I heard their voices under the ground, and one of them said: "Go and see if he is crying." And I heard rattles, but all the time they were outside the sacred place and could not get in, for I had resolved not to be afraid, and did not stop sending my voice to *Wakan-Tanka* for aid. Then later, one of the bad spirits said from somewhere under the ground: "Yes, he is surely crying," and the next morning I saw that the poles and offerings were still there. I was well prepared, you see, and did not weaken, and so nothing bad could happen.

The "lamenter" should get up in the middle of the night, and he should again go to the four quarters, returning to the center each time, and all the while he should be sending his voice. He should always be up with the morning star, and he should walk towards the east, and, pointing his pipe stem towards this sacred star, he should ask it for wisdom; this he should pray silently in his heart, and not out loud. All this the "lamenter" should do for the three or four days.

At the end of this period the helpers come with their horses and take the "lamenter" with his pipe back to the camp, and there he immediately enters the *Inipi* which has already been made ready for him. He should sit at the west, holding his pipe in front of him all the time. The holy man—the spiritual guide of the "lamenter"—enters next and, passing behind the "lamenter," sits at the east, and all the other men fill the remaining places.

The first sacred rock, which has already been heated, is brought into the lodge and is placed at the center of the altar, and then all the other rocks are brought in, as I have described before. All this is done very solemnly but more rapidly than before, for all the men are anxious to hear what the "lamenter" has to tell and to know what great things may have come to him up there on the mountain. When all has been made ready, the holy man says to the "lamenter":

"Ho! You have now sent a voice with your pipe to *Wakan-*

Little Warrior, 1947 *(Photograph by J. E. Brown)*

Tanka. That pipe is now very sacred, for the whole universe has seen it. You have offered this pipe to all the four sacred Powers; they have seen it! And each word that you said up there was heard, even by our Grandmother and Mother Earth. The coming generations will hear you! These five ancient rocks here will hear you! The winged Power of the place where the sun goes down, who controls the waters, will hear you! The standing trees who are present here will hear you! And also the most sacred pipe which was given to the people will hear you; so tell us the truth, and be sure that you make up nothing! Even the tiny ants and the crawling worms may have come to see you up there when you were crying for a vision; tell us everything! You have brought back to us the pipe which you offered; it is finished! And since you are about to put this pipe to your mouth, you should tell us nothing but the truth. The pipe is *wakan* and knows all things; you cannot fool it. If you lie, *Wakinyan-Tanka,* who guards the pipe, will punish you! *Hechetu welo!"*

The holy man rises from his position at the east and, moving around the lodge sun-wise, sits just at the right of the "lamenter." Dried buffalo chips are placed in front of the "lamenter," and upon these the pipe is placed with its stem pointing towards the heavens. The holy man now takes the tallow seal off the bowl of the pipe and places it upon the buffalo chips. He lights the pipe with a coal from the fire and, after offering it up to the Powers of the six directions, points the stem towards the "lamenter," who just touches it with his mouth. The holy man then makes a circle in the air with the stem of the pipe, smokes it a little himself, and again touches it to the mouth of the "lamenter." Then he again waves the pipe stem in a circle and again smokes it a little himself. This is done four times, and then the pipe is passed around the circle for all the men to smoke. When it returns to the holy man, with four motions he empties it upon the top of the tallow seal and the buffalo chips and then purifies it. Holding the pipe up in front of himself, the holy man says to the "lamenter": "Young man, you left here three days ago with your two helpers, who have set up for you the five posts upon the sacred place. Tell us everything that happened to you up there after these helpers left! Do not omit anything! We have prayed much to *Wakan-Tanka* for you and have asked the pipe to be merciful. Tell us now what happened!"

The "lamenter" replies, and after each time he says something of importance all the men in the lodge cry *"Hi ye!"*

"I went up on the mountain, and, after entering the sacred place, I walked continually to each of the four directions, always returning to the center as you had instructed me. During the first day, as I was facing the place where the sun goes down, I saw an eagle flying towards me, and when it came nearer I saw that it was a sacred Spotted Eagle. He rested on a tree near me but said nothing; and then he flew away to the place where the Giant *Waziah* lives."

To this all the men cry: *"Hi ye!"*

"I returned to the center, and then I went to the north, and as I stood there I saw an eagle circling above, and as he lighted near me I noticed that he was a young eagle, but it, too, said nothing to me, and soon he circled and soared off towards the place towards which we always face.

"I went back to the center where I cried and sent my voice, and then I went towards the place where the sun comes up. There I saw something flying towards me, and soon I saw that it was a baldheaded eagle, but he too said nothing to me.

"Crying, I returned to the center, and then when I went towards the place which we always face, I saw a red-breasted woodpecker standing on the offering pole. I believe he may have given to me something of his *wochangi,* for I heard him say to me very faintly yet distinctly: 'Be attentive! [*wachin ksapa yo!*] and have no fear; but pay no attention to any bad thing that may come and talk to you!' "

All the men now say more loudly: *"Hi ye!";* for this message which the bird gave is very important.

The "lamenter" continues: "Although I was crying and sending my voice continually, this was all that I heard and saw that first day. Then night fell, and I lay down with my head at the center and went to sleep; and in my sleep I heard and saw my people, and I noticed that they were all very happy.

"I arose in the middle of the night, and again walked to each of the four directions, returning to the center each time, continually sending my voice. Just before the morning star came up, I again visited the four quarters, and just as I reached the place where the sun rises, I saw the Morning Star, and I noticed that at first it was all red, and then it changed to blue, and then into yellow, and finally I saw that it was white, and in these four colors I saw the four ages. Although this star did not really speak to me, yet it taught me very much.

"I stood there waiting for the sun to rise, and just at dawn I saw the world full of little winged people, and they were all rejoicing. Finally the sun came up, bringing its light into the world, and then I began to cry and returned to the center where I lay down, leaning my pipe against the center offering-pole.

"As I lay there at the center I could hear all sorts of little wingeds who were sitting on the poles, but none of them spoke to me. I looked at my pipe and there I saw two ants walking on the stem. Perhaps they wished to speak to me, but soon they left.

"Often during the day as I was crying and sending my voice, birds and butterflies would come to me, and once a white butterfly came and sat on the end of the pipe stem, working his beautiful wings up and down. During this day I saw no large four-leggeds, just the little peoples. Then just before the sun went down to rest, I saw that clouds were gathering, and the Thunder-beings were coming. The lightning was all over the sky, and the thunder was terrifying, and I think that perhaps I was a little afraid. But I held my pipe up and continued to send my voice to *Wakan-Tanka;* and soon I heard another voice saying: '*Hee-ay-hay-ee-ee! Hee-ay-hay-ee-ee!*' Four times they said this, and then all the fear left me, for I remembered what the little bird had told me, and I felt very brave. I heard other voices, also, which I could not understand. I stood there with my eyes closed—I do not know how long —and when I opened them everything was very bright, brighter even than the day; and I saw many people on horseback coming towards me, all riding horses of different colors. One of the riders even spoke to me saying: 'Young man, you are offering the pipe to *Wakan-Tanka;* we are all very happy that you are doing this!' This is all that they said, and then they disappeared.

"The next day, just before the sun came up, as I was visiting the four quarters, I saw the same little red-breasted bird; he was sitting on the pole there where we always face, and he said almost the same thing to me as before: 'Friend, be attentive as you walk!' That was all. Soon after this the two helpers came to bring me back. This is all that I know; I have told the truth and have made nothing up!"

Thus the "lamenter" finishes his account. Now the holy man gives to him his pipe, which he embraces, and it is then passed around the circle, and a helper takes it and leans it, with its stem to the west, against the sacred mound at the east of the lodge. More hot rocks are handed into the lodge; the door is closed; and the *Inipi* begins.

The holy man prays, giving thanks to *Wakan-Tanka*: *"Hee-ey-hay-ee-ee!* [four times] O Grandfather, *Wakan-Tanka,* today You have helped us. You have been merciful to this young man by giving him knowledge and a path which he may follow. You have made his people happy, and all the beings who move in the universe are rejoicing!

"Grandfather, this young man who has offered the pipe to You, has heard a voice which said to him, 'be attentive as you walk!' He wants to know what this message means; it must now be explained to him. It means that he should always remember You, O *Wakan-Tanka,* as he walks the sacred path of life; and he must be attentive to all the signs that You have given to us. If he does this always, he will become wise and a leader of his people. O *Wakan-Tanka,* help us all to be always attentive![5]

[5] This message—"Be attentive!"—well expresses a spirit which is central to the Indian peoples; it implies that in every act, in every thing, and in every instant, the Great Spirit is present, and that one should be continually and intensely "attentive" to this Divine presence.

This presence of *Wakan-Tanka,* and one's consciousness of it, is that which the Christian saints have termed "living in the moment," the "eter-

"This young man also saw four ages in that star there where the sun comes up. These are the ages through which all creatures must pass in their journey from birth to death.

"O *Wakan-Tanka,* when this young man saw the dawn of the day, he saw Your light coming into the universe; this is the light of wisdom. All these things You have revealed to us, for it is Your will that the peoples of the world do not live in the darkness of ignorance.

"O *Wakan-Tanka,* You have established a relationship with this young man; and through this relationship he will bring strength to his people. We who are now sitting here represent all the people, and thus we all give thanks to You, O *Wakan-Tanka.* We all raise our hands to You and say: '*Wakan-Tanka,* we thank you for this understanding and relationship which you have given to us.' Be merciful to us always! May this relationship exist until the very end!"

All the men now sing this sacred chant.

Grandfather, behold me!
Grandfather, behold me!
I held my pipe and offered it to You,
That my people may live!

---

nal now," or what in the Islamic tradition is termed the *Waqt.* In Lakota this presence is called *Taku Skanskan,* or simply *Skan* in the sacred language of the holy men. The following conversation between the Lakota priest Finger and J. R. Walker well explains this:

" 'What causes the stars to fall?' '*Taku Skanskan.* . . . He causes everything that falls to fall, and He causes everything to move that moves.' 'When you move, what is it that causes you to move?' '*Skan.*' 'If an arrow is shot from a bow what causes it to move through the air?' '*Skan.* . . . Taku Skanskan* gives the spirit to the bow, and He causes it to send the arrow from it.' 'What causes smoke to go upward?' '*Taku Skanskan.*' 'What causes water to flow in a river?' '*Skan.*' 'What causes the clouds to move over the world?' '*Skan.*' 'Lakota have told me that *Skan* is the sky. Is that so?' 'Yes. *Skan* is a Spirit and all that mankind can see of Him is the blue of the sky; but He is everywhere!' 'Is *Skan Wakan-Tanka?*' 'Yes!' " (*The Sun Dance . . . of the Teton Dakota* [Anthropological Papers of the American Museum of Natural History, XVI, Part II].)

Grandfather, behold me!
Grandfather, behold me!
I give to You all these offerings,
That my people may live!

Grandfather, behold me!
Grandfather, behold me!
We who represent all the people,
Offer ourselves to You,
That we may live!

After this chant, water is put on the rocks, and the *Inipi* is continued in the same manner that I have described before. This young man who has cried for a vision for the first time, may perhaps become *wakan;* if he walks with his mind and heart attentive to *Wakan-Tanka* and His Powers, as he has been instructed, he will certainly travel upon the red path which leads to goodness and holiness. But he must cry for a vision a second time, and this time the bad spirits may tempt him; but if he is really a chosen one, he will stand firmly and will conquer all distracting thoughts and will become purified from all that is not good. Then he may receive some great vision that will bring strength to the nation. But should the young man still be in doubt after his second "lamenting," he may try a third and even a fourth time; and if he is always sincere, and truly humiliates himself before all things, he shall certainly be aided, for *Wakan-Tanka* always helps those who cry to Him with a pure heart.

CHAPTER V

Wiwanyag Wachipi: THE SUN DANCE

The *wiwanyag wachipi* (dance looking at the sun) is one of our greatest rites and was first held many, many winters after our people received the sacred pipe from the White Buffalo Cow Woman. It is held each year during the Moon of Fattening (June) or the Moon of Cherries Blackening (July), always at the time when the moon is full, for the growing and dying of the moon reminds us of our ignorance which comes and goes; but when the moon is full it is as if the eternal light of the Great Spirit were upon the whole world. But now I will tell you how this holy rite first came to our people and how it was first made.

Our people were once camped in a good place, in a circle, of course, and the old men were sitting having a council, when they noticed that one of our men, Kablaya (Spread), had dropped his robe down around his waist, and was dancing there all alone with

67

his hand raised towards heaven. The old men thought that perhaps he was crazy, so they sent someone to find out what was the
matter; but this man who was sent suddenly dropped his robe
down around his waist, too, and started dancing with Kablaya.
The old men thought this very strange, and so they all went over
to see what could be the matter. Kablaya then explained to them:

"Long ago *Wakan-Tanka* told us how to pray with the sacred
pipe, but we have now become lax in our prayers, and our people
are losing their strength. But I have just been shown, in a vision,
a new way of prayer; in this manner *Wakan-Tanka* has sent aid
to us."

When they heard this the old men all said, *"How!"* and seemed
very pleased. They then had a conference and sent two men to the
keeper of the sacred pipe, for he should give advice on all matters
of this sort. The keeper told the men that this was certainly a very
good thing, for "we were told that we would have seven ways of
praying to *Wakan-Tanka,* and this must certainly be one of them,
for Kablaya has been taught in a vision, and we were told in the
beginning that we should receive our rites in this manner."

The two messengers brought this news back to the old men,
who then asked Kablaya to instruct them in what they must do.
Kablaya then spoke to the men, saying: "This is to be the sun
dance; we cannot make it immediately but must wait four days,
and during this time we shall prepare, as I have been instructed
in my vision. This dance will be an offering of our bodies and
souls to *Wakan-Tanka* and will be very *wakan.* All our old and
holy men should gather; a large tipi should be built and sage
should be placed all around inside it. You must have a good pipe,
and also all the following equipment:

Ree twist tobacco	a tanned buffalo calf hide
bark of the red willow	rabbit skins
Sweet grass	eagle plumes
a bone knife	red earth paint
a flint axe	blue paint
buffalo tallow	rawhide

a buffalo skull   eagle tail feathers

a rawhide bag   whistles from the wing bones

of the Spotted Eagle.

After the people had secured all these sacred things, Kablaya then asked all those who could sing to come to him that evening so that he could teach them the holy songs; he said that they should bring with them a large drum made from a buffalo hide, and they should have very stout drum sticks, covered at the end with buffalo hide, the hair side out.

Since the drum is often the only instrument used in our sacred rites, I should perhaps tell you here why it is especially sacred and important to us. It is because the round form of the drum represents the whole universe, and its steady strong beat is the pulse, the heart, throbbing at the center of the universe. It is as the voice of *Wakan-Tanka,* and this sound stirs us and helps us to understand the mystery and power of all things.

That evening the singers, four men and a woman, came to Kablaya, who spoke to them in this manner: "O you, my relatives, for a very long time we have been sending our voices to *Wakan-Tanka.* This He has taught us to do. We have many ways of praying to Him, and through this sacred manner of living our generations have learned to walk the red path with firm steps. The sacred pipe is always at the center of the hoop of our nation, and with it the people have walked and will continue to walk in a holy manner.

"In this new rite which I have just received, one of the standing peoples has been chosen to be at our center; he is the *wagachun* (the rustling tree, or cottonwood); he will be our center and also the people, for the tree represents the way of the people. Does it not stretch from the earth here to heaven there?[1] This new way of sending our voices to *Wakan-Tanka* will be very powerful; its use will spread, and, at this time of year, every year, many people will

---

[1] In the *Atharva Veda Samhita* of the Hindu scriptures, we find a description of the significance of their World Tree, which is quite identical to the symbolism of the tree for the Lakota: "The World Tree in which the trunk, which is also the sun pillar, sacrificial post, and *axis mundi,*

pray to the Great Spirit. Before I teach you the holy songs, let us first offer the pipe to our Father and Grandfather, *Wakan-Tanka*."

"O Grandfather, Father, *Wakan-Tanka,* we are about to fulfill Thy will as You have taught us to do in my vision. This we know will be a very sacred way of sending our voices to You; through this, may our people receive wisdom; may it help us to walk the sacred path with all the Powers of the universe! Our prayer will really be the prayer of all things, for all are really one; all this I have seen in my vision. May the four Powers of the universe help us to do this rite correctly; O Great Spirit, have mercy upon us!"

The pipe was smoked by all, and then Kablaya began to teach the songs to the five people. Many other people had gathered around the singers, and to these Kablaya said that while they listen they should frequently cry "O Grandfather, *Wakan-Tanka,* I offer the pipe to You that my people may live!"

There were no words to the first song that Kablaya taught the singers; it was simply a chant, repeated four times, and the fast beat on the drum was used. The words to the second song were:

> *Wakan-Tanka, have mercy on us,*
> *That our people may live!*

And the third song was:

> *They say a herd of buffalo is coming;*
> *It is here now!*
> *Their blessing will come to us.*
> *It is with us now!*

The fourth song was a chant and had no words.

---

rising from the altar at the navel of the earth, penetrates the world door and branches out above the roof of the world (A. V. X. 7. 3.); as the 'non-existent (unmanifested) branch that yonder kindreds know as the Supernal' (A. V. X. 7. 21)." (Translated by A. K. Coomaraswamy, Svayamatrna: Janua Coeli," *Zalmoxis.*)

For a full explanation of the symbolism of the tree, see René Guénon, *Le Symbolisme de la Croix,* Les Editions Vega (Paris, 1931); especially Chap. IX, "L'Arbre du Milieu."

Then Kablaya taught the men who had brought their eagle-bone whistles how they should be used, and he also told the men what equipment they should prepare and explained the meaning of each ritual object.

"You should prepare a necklace of otter skin, and from it there should hang a circle with a cross in the center. At the four places where the cross meets the circle there should hang eagle feathers which represent the four Powers of the universe and the four ages. At the center of the circle you should tie a plume taken from the breast of the eagle, for this is the place which is nearest to the heart and center of the sacred bird. This plume will be for *Wakan-Tanka,* who dwells at the depths of the heavens, and who is the center of all things.

"You all have the eagle-bone whistles, and to the ends of each of these an eagle plume should be tied. When you blow the whistle always remember that it is the voice of the Spotted Eagle; our Grandfather, *Wakan-Tanka,* always hears this, for you see it is really His own voice.

"A *hanhepi wi* [night sun, or moon] should be cut from raw-hide in the shape of a crescent, for the moon represents a person and, also, all things, for everything created waxes and wanes, lives and dies. You should also understand that the night represents ignorance, but it is the moon and the stars which bring the Light of *Wakan-Tanka* into this darkness. As you know the moon comes and goes, but *anpetu wi,* the sun, lives on forever; it is the source of light, and because of this it is like *Wakan-Tanka.*

"A five-pointed star should be cut from rawhide. This will be the sacred Morning Star who stands between the darkness and the light, and who represents knowledge.

"A round rawhide circle should be made to represent the sun, and this should be painted red; but at the center there should be a round circle of blue, for this innermost center represents *Wakan-Tanka* as our Grandfather. The light of this sun enlightens the entire universe; and as the flames of the sun come to us in the morning, so comes the grace of *Wakan-Tanka,* by which all creatures are enlightened. It is because of this that the four-leggeds and the wingeds always rejoice at the coming of the light. We can all see in the day, and this seeing is sacred for it represents the sight of that real world which we may have through the eye of the heart. When you wear this sacred sign in the dance, you should remember that you are bringing Light into the universe, and if you concentrate on these meanings you will gain great benefit.

"A round circle should be cut and painted red, and this will represent Earth. She is sacred, for upon Her we place our feet, and from Her we send our voices to *Wakan-Tanka*. She is a relative of ours, and this we should always remember when we call Her "Grandmother" or "Mother." When we pray we raise our hand to the heavens, and afterwards we touch the earth, for is not our Spirit from *Wakan-Tanka*, and are not our bodies from the earth? We are related to all things: the earth and the stars, everything, and with all these together we raise our hand to *Wakan-Tanka* and pray to Him alone.

"You should also cut from rawhide another round circle, and this should be painted blue for the heavens. When you dance you should raise your head and hand up to these heavens, looking at them, for if you do this your Grandfather will see you. It is He who owns everything; there is nothing which does not belong to Him, and thus it is to Him alone that you should pray.

"Finally, you should cut from rawhide the form of *tatanka*, the buffalo. He represents the people and the universe and should always be treated with respect, for was he not here before the two-legged peoples, and is he not generous in that he gives us our homes and our food? The buffalo is wise in many things, and, thus, we should learn from him and should always be as a relative with him.

"Each man should wear one of these sacred symbols on his chest, and he should realize their meanings as I have explained to you here. In this great rite you are to offer your body as a sacrifice in behalf of all the people, and through you the people will gain understanding and strength. Always be conscious of these things which I have told you today; it is all *wakan!*"

The next day it was necessary to locate the sacred rustling tree which was to stand at the center of the great lodge, and so Kablaya told his helper of the type of tree which he should find and mark with sage, that the war party will be able to locate it and bring it back to camp. Kablaya also instructed the helpers how they must mark out the ground where the sacred sun-dance lodge will be set up, around the holy tree, and how they should mark the doorway at the east with green branches.

The following day the scouts, who had been chosen by the spiritual leaders, went out and pretended to scout for the tree. When it was found they returned immediately to camp, and after circling sun-wise around the place where the lodge was to be, they all charged for the doorway, trying to strike a coup on it. These scouts then took up a pipe, and, after offering it to the six directions, they swore that they would tell the truth. When this had been done, Kablaya spoke to the men in this manner:

"You have taken up the holy pipe, and so you must now tell us with truth all that you have seen. You know that running through the stem of the pipe there is a little hole leading straight to the center and heart of the pipe; let your minds be as straight as this Way. May your tongues not be forked. You have been sent out to find a tree that will be of great benefit to the people, so now tell us truthfully what you have found."

Kablaya then turned the pipe around four times, and pointed the stem towards the scout who was to give the report.

"I went over a hill, and there I saw many of the sacred standing peoples."

"In which direction were you facing, and what did you see beyond the first hill?"

"I was facing the west," the scout replied, "and then I went further and looked over a second hill and saw many more of the sacred standing people living there."

In this manner the scout was questioned four times, for as you know with our people all good things are done in fours; and then this is the manner in which we always question our scouts when we are on the warpath, for you see we are here regarding the tree as an enemy who is to be killed.

When the scouts had given their report, they all dressed as if they were going on the warpath; and then they left the camp as if to attack the enemy. Many other people followed behind the scouts. When they came to the chosen tree, they all gathered around it; then, last of all, Kablaya arrived with his pipe, which he held with its stem pointing towards the tree; he spoke in this manner:

"Of all the many standing peoples, you O rustling cottonwood have been chosen in a sacred manner; you are about to go to the center of the people's sacred hoop, and there you will represent the people and will help us to fulfill the will of *Wakan-Tanka*. You are a kind and good-looking tree; upon you the winged peoples have raised their families; from the tip of your lofty branches down to your roots, the winged and four-legged peoples have made their homes. When you stand at the center of the sacred hoop you will be the people, and you will be as the pipe, stretching from heaven to earth. The weak will lean upon you, and for all the people you will be a support. With the tips of your branches you hold the sacred red and blue days. You will stand where the four sacred paths cross—there you will be the center of the great Powers of the universe. May we two-leggeds always follow your sacred example, for we see that you are always looking upwards into the heavens. Soon, and with all the peoples of the world, you will stand at the center; for all beings and all things you will bring that which is good. *Hechetu welo!*"

Kablaya then offered his pipe to Heaven and Earth, and then with the stem he touched the tree on the west, north, east, and south sides; after this he lit and smoked the pipe.

I think it would be good to explain to you here why we consider the cottonwood tree to be so very sacred. I might mention first, that long ago it was the cottonwood who taught us how to make our tipis, for the leaf of the tree is an exact pattern of the tipi, and this we learned when some of our old men were watching little children making play houses from these leaves. This too is a good example of how much grown men may learn from very little children, for the hearts of little children are pure, and, therefore, the Great Spirit may show to them many things which older people miss. Another reason why we choose the cottonwood tree to be at the center of our lodge is that the Great Spirit has shown to us that, if you cut an upper limb of this tree crosswise, there you will see in the grain a perfect five pointed star, which, to us, represents the presence of the Great Spirit. Also perhaps you have noticed that even in the very lightest breeze you can hear the voice of the cottonwood tree; this we understand is its prayer to the Great Spirit,[2] for not only men, but all things and all beings pray to Him continually in differing ways.

The chiefs then did a little victory dance there around the tree, singing their chief's songs, and as they sang and danced they selected the man who was to have the honor of counting coup on the tree; he must always be a man of good character, who has shown himself brave and self-sacrificing on the warpath. Three other men were also chosen by the chiefs, and then each of these four men stood at one of the four sides of the tree—the leader at the west. This leader then told of his great deeds in war, and when he had finished the men cheered and the women gave the tremulo. The brave man then motioned with his axe three times towards the tree, and the fourth time he struck it. Then the other three men in turn told of their exploits in war, and when they finished they also struck the tree in the same manner, and at each blow all the people shouted *"hi! hey!"* When the tree was nearly ready to fall, the chiefs went around and selected a person with a quiet and holy nature, and this person gave the last blow to the tree; as it fell there was much cheering, and all the women gave the tremulo. Great care was taken that the tree did not touch the ground when it fell, and no one was permitted to step over it.

The tree was then carried by six men towards the camp, but before they reached camp they stopped four times, and after the

[2] An interesting parallel to this attitude towards trees is found in an Islamic source: "[Holy] men dance and wheel on the [spiritual] battlefield: From within them musicians strike the tambourine: at their ecstacy the seas burst into foam. You see it not, but for *their* ears the leaves too on the boughs are clapping hands. . . . one must have the spiritual ear, not the ear of the body." (Jalaluddin Rumi, *The Mathnawi* [R. A. Nicholson translation, 8 vols., Cambridge University Press, Cambridge, 1926], III 9.)

last stop they all howled like coyotes—as do the warriors when returning from the war path; then they all charged into camp and placed the sacred tree up upon poles—for it must not touch the ground—and pointed its base towards the hole which had already been prepared, and its tip faced towards the west. The lodge around the tree had not yet been set up, but all the poles had been prepared, and all the equipment for constructing the *Inipi* had been gathered.

The chief priest, Kablaya, and all those who were to take part in the dance, then went into a large tipi where they were to prepare themselves and receive instructions. The lodge was shut up very tightly, and leaves were even placed all around the base.

Kablaya, who was seated at the west, scraped a bare place on the ground in front of him, and here a coal was placed; as Kablaya burned sweet grass upon the coal, he said: "We burn this sacred herb for *Wakan-Tanka*, so that all the two-legged and winged peoples of the universe will be relatives and close to each other. Through this there shall be much happiness."

A small image of a drying rack was then made from two forked sticks and one straight one, and all were painted blue, for the drying rack represents heaven, and it is our prayer that the racks always be as full as heaven. The pipe was then taken up, and after being purified over the smoke, it was leaned against the rack, for in this way it represents our prayers and is the path leading from earth to heaven.

All the sacred things to be used in the dance were then purified over the smoke of the sweet grass: the hide figures; the sacred paints; the calf skin; and the buckskin bags; and the dancers, also, purified themselves. When this had been done, Kablaya took up his pipe, and, raising it to heaven, he prayed.

"O Grandfather, *Wakan-Tanka,* You are the maker of everything. You have always been and always will be. You have been kind to your people, for You have taught us a way of prayer with the pipe which You have given us; and now through a vision You have shown to me a sacred dance which I must teach to my people. Today we will do Thy will."

"As I stand upon this sacred earth, upon which generations of our people have stood, I send a voice to You by offering this pipe. Behold me, O *Wakan-Tanka,* for I represent all the people. Within this pipe I shall place the four Powers and all the wingeds of the universe; together with all these, who shall become one, I send a voice to You. Behold me! Enlighten my mind with Your never fading Light!"

"I offer this pipe to *Wakan-Tanka,* first through You O winged Power of the place where the sun goes down; there is a place for You in this pipe. Help us with those red and blue days which make the people holy!"

Kablaya then held up a pinch of tobacco, and after motioning with it to Heaven, Earth, and the four Powers, he placed it in the bowl of the pipe. Then after the following prayers, he placed pinches of tobacco in the pipe for each of the other directions.

"O winged Power of the place where *Waziah* lives, I am about to offer this pipe to *Wakan-Tanka;* help me with the two good red and blue days which You have—days which are purifying to the people and to the universe. There is a place for You in the pipe, and so help us!

"O You, Power there where the sun comes up; You who give knowledge and who guard the dawn of the day, help us with Your two red and blue days which give understanding and Light to the people. There is a place for You in this pipe which I am about to offer to *Wakan-Tanka;* help us!

"O You, most sacred Power at the place where we always face; You who are the source of life, and who guard the people and the coming generations, help us with Your two red and blue days! There is a place for You in the pipe.

"O You, Spotted Eagle of the heavens! we know that You have sharp eyes with which you see even the smallest object that moves on Grandmother Earth. O You, who are in the depths of the heavens, and who know everything, I am offering this pipe to *Wakan-Tanka!* Help us with Your two good red and blue days!

"O You, Grandmother Earth, who lie outstretched, supporting all things! upon You a two-legged is standing, offering a pipe to the Great Spirit. You are at the center of the two good red and blue days. There will be a place for You in the pipe and so help us!"

Kablaya then placed a small grain of tobacco in the pipe for each of the following birds: the kingbird; the robin; the lark, who sings during the two good days; the woodpecker; the hawk, who makes life so difficult for the other winged peoples; the eagle hawk; the magpie, who knows everything; the blackbird; and many other wingeds. Now all objects of creation and the six directions of space have been placed within the bowl of the pipe. The pipe was sealed with tallow and was leaned against the little blue drying rack.

Kablaya then took up another pipe, filled it, and went to where the sacred tree was resting. A live coal was brought, and the tree and the hole were purified with the smoke from sweet grass.

"O *Wakan-Tanka*," Kablaya prayed as he held his pipe up with one hand, "behold this holy tree-person who will soon be placed in this hole. He will stand with the sacred pipe. I touch him with the sacred red earth paint from our Grandmother and also with the fat from the four-legged buffalo. By touching this tree-person with the red earth, we remember that the generations of all that move come from our Mother the Earth. With your help, O tree, I shall soon offer my body and soul to *Wakan-Tanka*, and in me I offer all my people and all the generations to come."

Kablaya then took the red paint, offered it to the six directions, and again spoke to the sacred tree: "O tree, you are about to stand up; be merciful to my people, that they may flourish under you."

Kablaya painted stripes of red on the west, north, east, and south sides of the tree, and then he touched a very little paint to the tip of the tree for the Great Spirit, and he also put some at the base of the tree for Mother Earth. Then Kablaya took up the skin of a buffalo calf, saying: "It is from this buffalo person that our people live; he gives to us our homes, our clothing, our food, everything we need. O buffalo calf, I now give to you a sacred place upon the tip of the tree. This tree will hold you in his hand and will raise you up to *Wakan-Tanka*. Behold what I am about to do! Through this, all things that move and fly upon the earth and in the heavens will be happy!"

Kablaya next held up a small cherry tree, and continued to pray: "Behold this, O *Wakan-Tanka,* for it is the tree of the people, which we pray will bear much fruit."

This little tree was then tied upon the sacred cottonwood, just below the buffalo hide, and with it there was tied a buckskin bag in which there was some fat.

Kablaya then took up the hide images of a buffalo and a man, and, offering them to the six directions, he prayed: "Behold this buffalo, O Grandfather, which You have given to us; he is the chief of all the four-leggeds upon our sacred Mother; from him the people live, and with him they walk the sacred path. Behold, too, this two-legged, who represents all the people. These are the two chiefs upon this great island; bestow upon them all the favours that they ask for, O *Wakan-Tanka!"*

These two images were then tied upon the tree, just underneath the place where the tree forks; after this Kablaya held up a bag of fat to be placed underneath the base of the tree, and he prayed in this manner:

"O Grandfather, *Wakan-Tanka,* behold this sacred fat, upon which this tree-person will stand; may the earth always be as fat and fruitful as this. O tree, this is a sacred day for you and for all our people; the earth within this hoop belongs to you, O tree, and it is here underneath you that I shall offer up my body and soul for the sake of the people. Here I shall stand, sending my voice to You, O *Wakan-Tanka,* as I offer the sacred pipe. All this may be difficult to do, yet for the good of the people it must be done. Help me, O Grandfather, and give to me courage and strength to stand the sufferings which I am about to undergo! O tree, you are now admitted to the sacred lodge!"

With much cheering and many shrill tremulos, the tree was raised, very slowly, for the men stopped four times before it was straight and dropped into the hole prepared for it. Now all the people—the two-leggeds, four-leggeds, and the wingeds of the air —were rejoicing, for they would all flourish under the protection of the tree. It helps us all to walk the sacred path; we can lean upon it, and it will always guide us and give us strength.

A little dance was held around the base of the tree, and then the surrounding lodge was made by putting upright, in a large circle, twenty-eight forked sticks, and from the fork of each stick a pole was placed which reached to the holy tree at the center.

I should explain to you here that in setting up the sun dance lodge, we are really making the universe in a likeness; for, you see, each of the posts around the lodge represents some particular object of creation, so that the whole circle is the entire creation, and the one tree at the center, upon which the twenty-eight poles rest, is *Wakan-Tanka,* who is the center of everything. Everything comes from Him, and sooner or later everything returns to Him. And I should also tell you why it is that we use twenty-eight poles. I have already explained why the numbers four and seven are sacred; then if you add four sevens you get twenty-eight. Also the moon lives twenty-eight days, and this is our month; each of these days of the month represents something sacred to us: two of the days represent the Great Spirit; two are for Mother Earth; four are for the four winds; one is for the Spotted Eagle; one for the sun; and one for the moon; one is for the Morning Star; and four for the four ages; seven are for our seven great rites; one is for the buffalo; one for the fire; one for the water; one for the rock; and finally one is for the two-legged people. If you add all these days up you will see that they come to twenty-eight. You should also know that the buffalo has twenty-eight ribs, and that in our war bonnets we usually use twenty-eight feathers. You see, there is a significance for everything, and these are the things that are good for men to know, and to remember. But now we must return to the sun dance.

The warriors all dressed and painted themselves, and after entering the sacred lodge they danced around the center tree, for in this way the ground was purified and made smooth by the dancing feet. The chiefs then gathered and selected braves, one of which was to be the leader of the dancers. These chosen men then danced first towards the west, and then back to the center, then to the

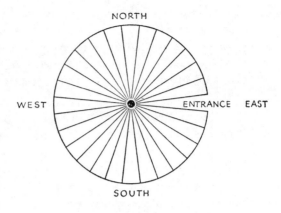

A Sun Dance Lodge

north and to the center, to the east and to the center, and finally to the south and then back to the center, and in this way they made a path in the shape of a cross.

Kablaya then entered the *Inipi* lodge, carrying the sacred pipe which had already been filled, and he sat at the west; all the other men who were to take part in the dance also entered, taking care not to pass in front of Kablaya, and then one woman entered last, taking her seat next to the door.

All the buffalo robes to be used in the dance were placed on top of the *Inipi* lodge, for in this way they are purified. The five hot rocks for the five directions were brought in and put in their proper places at the sacred altar, and then a sixth rock was placed upon the sacred path.

81

Kablaya held that pipe which was to be used in the dance, but a second pipe which to be used for the rites of the *Inipi* was filled and was handed to Kablaya to bless and to light. This pipe was smoked around the circle in the ritual manner, purified by Kablaya, and was then handed out of the lodge. The door was closed, and now it was the time for Kablaya to explain his vision to the people.

"My relatives all—listen! *Wakan-Tanka* has been kind to us, and has placed us upon a sacred Earth; upon Her we are now sitting. You have just seen the five sacred rocks placed here at the center, and that sixth rock which was placed upon the path represents the people. For the good of you all *Wakan-Tanka* has taught to me in a vision, a way of worship—this I am now teaching to you.

"The heavens are sacred, for it is there that our Grandfather, the Great Spirit, lives; these heavens are as a cloak for the universe—this robe is now upon me as I stand here. O *Wakan-Tanka*, I show to You the sacred hoop of our nation, which is this circle within which there is a cross; this circle one of us wears upon his breast. And I show to You the earth which You have made, and which You are always making; it is represented by this round red circle which we wear. The never-ending Light which turns the night into day, we also wear, that the Light may be amongst our people, that they may see. I show to You also the Morning Star which gives knowledge to us. The four-legged buffalo whom You have placed here before the two-legged people is also here with us. And here is also the sacred woman who came to us in such a holy manner. All these holy peoples and holy things are now hearing what I say!

"Very soon I shall suffer and endure great pain with my relatives here, in behalf of my people. In tears and suffering I shall hold my pipe and raise my voice to You, O *Wakan-Tanka*. I shall offer up my body and soul that my people may live. In sending my voice to You, *Wakan-Tanka*, I shall use that which connects the four Powers, Heaven, and Earth, to You. All that which moves on the universe—the four-leggeds, the insects, and the wingeds—all rejoice and help me and all my people!"

Kablaya then sang his sacred song:

The Sun, the Light of the world,
I hear Him coming.
I see His face as He comes.
He makes the beings on earth happy,
And they rejoice.
O Wakan-Tanka, *I offer to You this world of Light.*

The pipe to be used in the sacred dance was then wrapped in sage and was taken out of the lodge by the woman; she carried it along the sacred path to the east and placed it upon the buffalo skull, being careful to have its stem point towards the east. This woman then remained outside the little lodge and assisted in opening and closing the door. The *Inipi* then began as I have described before, but after the second time the door was closed, Kablaya made a special prayer in this manner:

"Grandfather, *Wakan-Tanka,* behold us! The sacred pipe which You have given to us, and with which we have raised our children, will soon go to the center of the universe, along with the buffalo, who has helped to make strong the bodies of the people. The sacred woman who once before came to the center of our hoop will again come to our center, and a two-legged who will suffer for his people will also go to the center. O *Wakan-Tanka,* when we are all at the center, may we have only You in our minds and hearts!"

Kablaya then sang another of the sacred songs which he had received in his vision.

I hear Him coming; I see His face.
Your day is sacred! I offer it to You.
I hear Him coming; I see His face.
This sacred day You made the buffalo roam.
You have made a happy day for the world;
I offer all to You.

Water was then put on the rocks as Kablaya prayed: "O *Wak-*

83

an-Tanka, we are now purifying ourselves, that we may be worthy to raise our hands to You."

Then raising their right hands, all the men sang.

> *Grandfather, I send my voice to You.*
> *Grandfather, I send my voice to You.*
> *With all the universe I send my voice to You,*
> *That I may live.*

When the door was opened the third time, the men were all allowed to drink a little water, but this was the only time during the whole rite that this was permitted. As the men received the water, Kablaya said to them: "I give you water, but remember the One in the west who guards the waters and the sanctity of all things. You are about to drink the water, which is life, and so you should not spill any of it. When you finish you should raise your hands in thanks to the Power of the place where the sun goes down; he will help you to bear the difficulties which you are about to undergo."

The door was closed for the last time, and again all the men sang as the heat and steam purified them. And when the door was finally opened, they all came out, led by Kablaya, and they raised their hands to the six directions, saying: *"Hi ho! Hi ho! Pila-miya!"* (thanks).

Each dancer had a helper, who took a purified buffalo robe from the top of the *Inipi* lodge and put it around the dancer. Kablaya then took his pipe which had been resting on the buffalo skull, and, with all the men, he entered a sacred tipi and placed his pipe against the little drying rack, which had been painted blue to represent the heavens. Sweet grass was put on a coal, and Kablaya and all the men purified themselves in the sacred smoke. After this, the drum and drumsticks were blessed and purified, and as he did this Kablaya said: "This drum is the buffalo and will go to the center. By using these sticks upon the drum, we shall certainly defeat our enemies."

All the clothing and equipment to be used in the dance were then purified; the four buffalo skulls were also purified, for one of the men would soon fasten these to his skin, bearing them in this way until they break loose.

Kablaya then explained to the men that their bodies had been purified and, thus were now sacred and should not even be touched by their own hands. The men must carry little sticks in their hair with which to scratch themselves, should it be necessary, and even when they paint themselves with the red earth paint they must use sticks instead of their hands.

Kablaya put around his neck the round blue hide circle representing the heavens, and each of the other men wore the different symbols: the circle with the cross; the red earth circle; the sun; the moon; and the Morning Star. The seventh man wore the buffalo, and the woman carried the pipe, for she represents the White Buffalo Cow Woman. The men also put rabbit skins on their arms and legs, for the rabbit represents humility, because he is quiet and soft and not self-asserting—a quality which we must all possess when we go to the center of the world. The men also put feathers in their hair, and, after these preparations, Kablaya instructed them in what they must do when they enter the sacred dance lodge.

"When we go to the center of the hoop we shall all cry, for we should know that anything born into this world which you see about you must suffer and bear difficulties. We are now going to suffer at the center of the sacred hoop, and by doing this may we take upon ourselves much of the suffering of our people."

Each of the men then declared which of the sacrifices he would undergo, and Kablaya made his vow first: "I will attach my body to the thongs of the Great Spirit which come down to earth—this shall be my offering."

(I think I should explain to you here, that the flesh represents ignorance, and, thus, as we dance and break the thong loose, it is as if we were being freed from the bonds of the flesh. It is much the same as when you break a young colt; at first a halter is necessary, but later when he has become broken, the rope is no longer necessary. We too are young colts when we start to dance, but soon we become broken and submit to the Great Spirit.)

85

The second dancer said: "I will tie myself to the four Powers of the world which *Wakan-Tanka* has established."

Here the dancer actually is the center—for standing at the center of four posts, rawhide thongs from these posts are tied into the flesh of his shoulders, his breast, and his back, and in this manner he dances until these thongs have broken out from his flesh.

The third dancer made his vow: "I will bear four of my closest relatives, the ancient buffalo."

By this the dancer means that four thongs will be tied into his back, to which will be attached four buffalo skulls, and these four bonds represent the pull of ignorance which should always be behind us as we face the light of truth which is before us.

The fourth dancer said: "I will leave twelve pieces of my flesh at the foot of the sacred tree. One shall be for *Wakan-Tanka,* our Grandfather, one for *Wakan-Tanka,* our Father, one for the Earth, our Grandmother, and one for the Earth, our Mother. I will leave four pieces of flesh for the Powers of the four directions, and then I will leave one for the Spotted Eagle, one for the Morning Star, one for the moon, and one for the sun."

The fifth dancer said: "I will make an offering of eight pieces of my flesh; two shall be for *Wakan-Tanka,* two for the Earth, and four for the Powers of the four directions."

The sixth dancer said: "I will leave at the sacred tree four pieces of my flesh; one shall be for *Wakan-Tanka,* one for the Earth upon whom we walk, one for the people that they may walk with firm steps, and one for the wingeds of the universe."

The seventh dancer made his vow: "I will leave one piece of my flesh for *Wakan-Tanka* and one for the Earth."

Then the eighth dancer, who was the woman, made her vow: "I will offer one piece of my flesh to *Wakan-Tanka* and for all moving things of the universe, that they may give their powers to the people, that they with their children may walk the red path of life."

When all had finished making their vows, Kablaya told them to purify themselves by rubbing sage on their faces and all over their bodies, "for we are now about to approach a sacred place where the tree stands, as the pipe, stretching from Heaven to Earth. We must be worthy to go to this center!"

All the people of the band had gathered around the outside of the sacred lodge, and within the lodge at the south were the singers, with the women who were their helpers, and all were wearing wreaths around their foreheads and holding little sprigs of some sacred plant.

Then the dancers arrived, being led by the woman, who carried the sacred pipe, and followed by Kablaya, carrying the buffalo skull, and at the end of the line were the helpers who carried all the equipment. They all walked slowly around the outside of the lodge, in a sun-wise direction, and all the time they were crying most pitifully: "O *Wakan-Tanka,* be merciful to me, that my people may live! It is for this that I am sacrificing myself."

And as the dancers chanted this, all the other people cried, for they were the people—the nation—for whom the dancers were to suffer. The dancers entered the lodge at the east and, after moving around the lodge sun-wise, took their places at the west. Then Kablaya placed the buffalo skull between the dancers and the sacred tree, with the nose of the skull facing the east; and just in front of him, he set up the three blue forked sticks, and upon this rack the woman rested the sacred pipe.

The singers then sang one of the sacred songs:

> Wakan-Tanka *be merciful to me. We want to live!*
> *That is why we are doing this.*
> *They say that a herd of buffalo is coming;*
> *Now they are here.*
> *The power of the buffalo is coming upon us;*
> *It is now here!"*

After the chanting of this song the people all cried, and then, for the rest of the day and all that night, they danced. This dance, during the first night, represents the people in the darkness of ignorance; they were not yet worthy to meet the Light of the Great Spirit which would shine upon them with the coming of the next

87

day; first they must suffer and purify themselves before they could be worthy to be with *Wakan-Tanka*.

Just before dawn, the dance stopped, and at this time the dancers, or their relatives, placed offerings outside the sacred lodge at each of the four quarters.

At dawn the dancers again entered the lodge, and with them there was the keeper of the sacred pipe; this holy man had been asked by Kablaya to make the sacred altar, but he had replied, "this is your vision Kablaya, and you should make the altar; but I will be present beside you, and when you have finished I will offer up the prayer."

Thus, it was Kablaya who made the sacred place; he first scraped a round circle in the ground in front of him, and then within this circle he placed a hot coal.[3] Then taking up some sweet grass and holding it above him, he prayed.

"O Grandfather, *Wakan-Tanka*, this is Your sacred grass which I place on the fire; its smoke will spread throughout the world, reaching even to the heavens. The four-leggeds, the wingeds, and all things will know this smoke and will rejoice. May this offering help to make all things and all beings as relatives to us; may they all give to us their powers, so that we may endure the difficulties ahead of us. Behold, O *Wakan-Tanka*, I place this sweet grass on the fire, and the smoke will rise to You."

As Kablaya placed the sacred grass on the fire, he sang this song:

> *I am making sacred smoke;*
> *In this manner I make the smoke;*
> *May all the peoples behold it!*
> *I am making sacred smoke;*

[3] This coal was taken from a fire which had been kept burning all through the previous night, and which will burn every night during the dance. It is located to the east, outside the lodge, and, according to Black Elk, it is kept in order to remind the people of the eternal presence of *Wakan-Tanka*. During the day this fire is not necessary because the sun is then present as a reminder.

Wiwanyag Wachipi: THE SUN DANCE

May all be attentive and behold!
May the wingeds, and the four-leggeds
be attentive and behold it!
In this manner I make the smoke;
All over the universe there will be rejoicing!

The knife which was to be used for piercing the breasts of the dancers was purified over the smoke, as was also a small stone hatchet and a small quantity of earth. Kablaya was then ready to make the sacred altar; but first he prayed.

"O Grandfather, *Wakan-Tanka,* I shall now make this Your sacred place. In making this altar, all the birds of the air and all creatures of the earth will rejoice, and they will come from all directions to behold it! All the generations of my people will rejoice! This place will be the center of the paths of the four great Powers. The dawn of the day will see this holy place! When Your Light approaches, O *Wakan-Tanka,* all that moves in the universe will rejoice!"

A pinch of the purified earth was offered above and to the ground and was then placed at the center of the sacred place. Another pinch of earth was offered to the west, north, east, and south and was placed at the west of the circle. In the same manner, earth was placed at the other three directions, and then it was spread evenly all around within the circle. This earth represents the two-leggeds, the four-leggeds, the wingeds, and really all that moves, and all that is in the universe. Upon this sacred place Kablaya then began to construct the altar. He first took up a stick, pointed it to the six directions, and then, bringing it down, he made a small circle at the center; and this we understand to be the home of *Wakan-Tanka.* Again, after pointing the stick to the six directions, Kablaya made a mark starting from the west and leading to the edge of the circle. In the same manner he drew a line from the east to the edge of the circle, from the north to the circle, and from the south to the circle. By constructing the altar in this manner, we see that everything leads into, or returns to, the center; ner, we see that everything leads into, or returns to, the center;

and this center which is here, but which we know is really everywhere, is *Wakan-Tanka.*

Kablaya then took up a small bundle of sage, and, offering it up to *Wakan-Tanka,* he prayed.

"O *Wakan-Tanka,* behold us! Next to the two-leggeds, the chief of all the four-leggeds is *tatanka,* the buffalo. Behold his dried skull here; by this we know that we, too, shall become skull and bones, and, thus, together we shall all walk the sacred path back to *Wakan-Tanka.* When we arrive at the end of our days, be merciful to us, O *Wakan-Tanka.* Here on earth we live together with the buffalo, and we are grateful to him, for it is he who gives us our food, and who makes the people happy. For this reason I now give grass to our relative the buffalo."

Kablaya then made a little bed of sage to the east of the sacred altar, and, taking up the buffalo skull by the horns, and facing the east, he sang:

> *I give grass to the buffalo;*
> *May the people behold it,*
> *That they may live.*

Then turning, and holding the skull to the west, Kablaya sang:

> *Tobacco I give to the buffalo;*
> *May the people behold it,*
> *That they may live.*

Then turning to the north, Kablaya sang:

> *A robe I give to the buffalo;*
> *May the people behold it,*
> *That they may live.*

And turning to the south he sang:

> *Paint I give to the buffalo;*
> *May the people behold it,*
> *That they may live.*

Then standing over the sage, Kablaya sang:

> *Water I will give to the buffalo;*
> *May the people behold it,*
> *That they may live.*

The buffalo skull was then placed on the bed of sage, facing east, and Kablaya placed little balls of sage in its eyes and tied a little bag of tobacco on the horn which was facing south, and he also tied a piece of deerhide on the horn at the north, for this hide represents the robe for the buffalo. Then Kablaya painted a red line around the head of the buffalo and drew, also, a red line from the forehead to the tip of the nose. As he did this Kablaya said: "You, O buffalo, are the earth! May we understand this, and all that I have done here. *Hechetu welo!* It is good!"

When the offerings to the buffalo had been completed, the dancers walked around the lodge and stood at the doorway facing east, in order to greet the rising sun.

"Behold these men, O *Wakan-Tanka,*" Kablaya prayed as he raised his right hand. "The face of the dawn will meet their faces; the coming day will suffer with them. It will be a sacred day, for You, O *Wakan-Tanka,* are present here!"

Then, just as the day-sun peeped over the horizon, the dancers all chanted in a sacred manner, and Kablaya sang one of his *wakan* songs.

> *The light of* Wakan-Tanka *is upon my people;*
> *It is making the whole earth bright.*
> *My people are now happy!*
> *All beings that move are rejoicing!*

As the men chanted, and as Kablaya sang the sacred song, they all danced, and as they danced they moved so that they were facing the south, then the west, the north, and then they stood again at the east; but this time they faced towards the sacred tree at the center.

The singing and drumming stopped, and the dancers sat at the west of the lodge, upon beds of sage which had been prepared for them. With sage the helpers rubbed all the paint off the men, and then upon their heads they placed wreaths of sage and plumes from the eagle, and the women also wore eagle feathers in their hair.

In every sun dance we wear wreaths of sage upon our heads, for it is a sign that our minds and hearts are close to *Wakan-Tanka* and His Powers, for the wreath represents the things of the heavens —the stars and planets, which are very mysterious and *wakan*.

Kablaya then told the dancers how they must paint themselves: the bodies were to be painted red from the waist up; the face, too, must be painted red, for red represents all that is sacred, especially the earth, for we should remember that it is from the earth that our bodies come, and it is to her that they return. A black circle should be painted around the face, for the circle helps us to remember *Wakan-Tanka,* who, like the circle, has no end. There is much power in the circle, as I have often said; the birds know this for they fly in a circle, and build their homes in the form of a circle; this the coyotes know also, for they live in round holes in the ground. Then a black line should be drawn from the forehead to a point between the eyes; and a line should be drawn on each cheek and on the chin, for these four lines represent the Powers of the four directions. Black stripes were painted around the wrists, the elbow, the upper part of the arm, and around the ankles. Black, you see, is the color of ignorance,[4] and, thus, these stripes are as the bonds which tie us to the earth. You should also notice that these stripes start from the earth and go up only as far as the breasts, for this is the place where the thongs fasten into the body, and these thongs are as rays of light from *Wakan-Tanka*. Thus, when we tear ourselves away from the thongs, it is as if the spirit were liberated from our dark bodies. At this first dance all the

[4] The Sioux also paint their faces black for the dance which is held when they return from the warpath, for, as Black Elk has said, "By going on the warpath, we know that we have done something bad, and we wish to hide our faces from *Wakan-Tanka.*"

Sitting Bull, 1885 *(Bureau of American Ethnology)*

men were painted in this manner; it is only in recent times that each dancer is painted with a different design, according to some vision which he may have had.

After all the dancers were painted, they purified themselves in the smoke of sweet grass and put on the various symbols which I have described before. The dancer who had vowed to drag the four buffalo skulls wore the form of the buffalo on his chest, and on his head he wore horns made from sage.

When all the preparations were finished, the dancers stood at the foot of the sacred tree, at the west, and, gazing up at the top of the tree, they raised their right hands and blew upon the eagle-bone whistles. As they did this, Kablaya prayed.

"O Grandfather, *Wakan-Tanka,* bend down and look upon me as I raise my hand to You. You see here the faces of my people. You see the four Powers of the universe, and You have now seen us at each of these four directions. You have beheld the sacred place and the sacred center which we have fixed, and where we shall suffer. I offer all my suffering to You in behalf of the people.

"A good day has been set upon my forehead as I stand before You, and this brings me closer to You, O *Wakan-Tanka.* It is Your light which comes with the dawn of the day, and which passes through the heavens. I am standing with my feet upon Your sacred Earth. Be merciful to me, O Great Spirit, that my people may live!"

Then all the singers chanted together:

> O Wakan-Tanka, *be merciful to me!*
> *I am doing this that my people may live!*

The dancers all moved around to the east, looking towards the top of the sacred tree at the west, and, raising up their hands, they sang:

> *Our Grandfather,* Wakan-Tanka,
> *has given to me a path which is sacred!*

Moving now to the south, and looking towards the north, the dancers blew upon their eagle-bone whistles, as the singers chanted:

A buffalo is coming they say.
He is here now.
The Power of the buffalo is coming;
It is upon us now!

As the singers chanted this, the dancers moved around to the west, and faced the east, and all the time they blew upon their shrill eagle-bone whistles. Then they went to the north and faced the south, and, finally, they again went to the west and faced towards the east.

Then the dancers all began to cry, and Kablaya was given a long thong and two wooden pegs, and with these he went to the center, and grasping the sacred tree he cried: "O *Wakan-Tanka*, be merciful to me. I do this that my people may live."

Crying in this manner continually, Kablaya went to the north of the lodge, and from there he walked around the circle of the lodge, stopping at each of the twenty-eight lodge poles, and then returned to the north. Carrying their thongs and pegs, all the dancers then did as Kablaya had done. When they all returned to the north and faced the south, Kablaya once again went to the center and grasped the sacred tree with both hands.

As the singers and drummers increased the speed of their chanting and drumming, the helpers rushed up and, grasping Kablaya roughly, threw him on the ground. The helper then pulled up the skin of Kablaya's left breast, and through this loose skin a sharp stick was thrust; and in the same manner the right breast was pierced. The long rawhide rope had been tied at its middle, around the sacred tree, towards its top, and then the two ends of the rope were tied to the pegs in Kablaya's chest. The helpers stood Kablaya up roughly, and he blew upon his eagle-bone whistle, and, leaning back upon his thongs, he danced, and continued to dance in this manner until the thongs broke loose from his flesh.

I should explain here why we use two thongs, which are really one long thong, for it is tied to the tree at its center, and also it

94

was made from a single buffalo hide, cut in a spiral. This is to help us remember that although there seem to be two thongs, the two are really only one; it is only the ignorant person who sees many where there is really only one. This truth of the oneness of all things we understand a little better by participating in this rite, and by offering ourselves as a sacrifice.

The second dancer then went to the center, and, grasping the sacred tree, he too cried as Kablaya had done. The helpers again rushed up and, after throwing him roughly on the ground, pierced both his breasts and both sides of his back; wooden pegs were thrust through the flesh, and to these pegs four short thongs were attached. This brave dancer was then tied at the center of four poles, so tightly that he could not move in any direction. At first he cried, not as a child from the pain, but because he knew that he was suffering for his people, and he was understanding the sacredness of having the four directions meet in his body, so that he himself was really the center. Raising his hands to heaven, and blowing upon his eagle whistle, this man danced until his thongs broke loose.

The third dancer who was to bear the four buffalo skulls then went to the center, and, after grasping the sacred tree, he was thrown on his face by the helpers, and four sticks were thrust through the flesh of his back. To these were tied the four buffalo skulls. The helpers pulled on the skulls to see that they were firmly attached, and then they gave to the dancer his eagle whistle, and upon this he blew continually as he danced. I think that you can understand that all this was very painful for him, for every time he moved the sharp horns of the skulls cut into his skin, but our men were brave in those days and did not show any signs of suffering; they were really glad to suffer if it was for the good of the people.

Friends or relatives would sometimes go to the dancers and dance beside them, giving encouragement; sometimes a young woman who liked one of the dancers would put a herb which she had been chewing into the mouth of the dancer in order to give him strength and to ease his thirst. And all this time the drumming, singing, and dancing never stopped, and above it all you could hear the shrill call of the eagle-bone whistles.

The fourth man, who had vowed to give twelve pieces of his flesh, then went and sat at the foot of the tree, holding on to it with both hands; the helpers took a bone awl and, raising up little pieces of flesh on the shoulders, cut off six small pieces from each. This flesh was left as an offering at the foot of the tree, and the man then stood up and continued dancing with the others.

In the same manner, the fifth dancer sacrificed eight pieces of his flesh; the sixth dancer gave four pieces of his flesh; and the seventh dancer sacrificed two pieces. Then, finally, the woman grasped the sacred tree, crying as she sat down, and said: "Father, *Wakan-Tanka,* in this one piece of flesh I offer myself to You and to Your heavens and to the sun, the moon, the Morning Star, the four Powers, and to everything."

They all continued to dance, and the people cheered Kablaya, telling him to pull harder upon the thongs, which he did until finally one thong broke loose, and then all the people cried *"hi ye!"* Kablaya fell, but the people helped him up, and he continued to dance until the other thong broke loose. Again he fell, but, rising, he raised both hands to heaven, and all the people cheered loudly. They then helped him to the foot of the sacred tree, where he rested on a bed of sage, and, pulling the loose flesh from his breast, where the bonds had broken loose, he placed twelve pieces of it at the foot of the tree. The medicine men put a healing herb on his wounds, and they carried him to a place in the shade where he rested for a few moments. Then, getting up, he continued to dance with the others.

Finally, the man who had been dancing for a long time with the four skulls lost two of them, and Kablaya gave the order that his skin should be cut so that the other two should break loose. But even though he was free from the four skulls, this brave man still continued to dance.

Then the man who had been dancing at the center of the four posts broke loose from two of his bonds, and Kablaya said that he, too, had had enough, and with a knife the skin was cut, so that he

broke loose from the other two bonds. These two men each offered twelve pieces of their flesh to the sacred tree, and then all the
men and many of the people continued to dance until the sun was
nearly down.

Just before sundown, a pipe was taken to the singers and drummers as an indication that their work had been finished and that
they may now smoke. Then the dancers and the keeper of the
most sacred pipe sat at the west of the lodge, and the holy woman
took up in her two hands the pipe which had been resting in front
of her; holding the stem of the pipe up, she walked around the
buffalo skull, and, standing in front of the keeper of the pipe, she
prayed.

"O holy Father, have pity on me! I offer my pipe to *Wakan-
Tanka.* O Grandfather, *Wakan-Tanka,* help me! I do this that
my people may live, and that they may increase in a sacred manner."

The woman then offered the pipe to the keeper three times,
and the fourth time she gave it to him. *"How!"* the keeper said
as he received the pipe; and then he went and stood under the
north side of the sacred tree and prayed.

"Hee-ay-hay-ee-ee! [four times] Grandfather, *Wakan-Tanka,*
You are closer to us than anything. You have seen everything this
day. It is now finished; our work has ended. Today a two-legged
person has made a very sacred rite, which You have appointed
him to do. These eight people here have offered their bodies and
souls to You. In suffering they have sent their voices to You; they
have even offered to You a part of their flesh, which is now here
at the foot of this sacred tree. The favor that they ask of You is
that their people may walk the holy path of life and that they may
increase in a sacred manner.

"Behold this pipe which we—with the Earth, the four Powers,
and with all things—have offered to You. We know that we are
related and are one with all things of the heavens and the earth,
and we know that all the things that move are a people as we. We
all wish to live and increase in a holy manner. The Morning Star
and the dawn which comes with it, the moon of the night, and

97

the stars of the heavens are all brought together here. You have taught us our relationship with all these things and beings, and for this we give thanks, now and always. May we be continually aware of this relationship which exists between the four-leggeds, the two-leggeds, and the wingeds. May we all rejoice and live in peace!

"Behold this pipe which is the one that the four-legged brought to the people; through it we have carried out Thy will. O *Wakan-Tanka,* You have put Your people upon a sacred path; may they walk upon it with firm and sure steps, hand in hand with their children, and may their children's children, too, walk in this sacred manner!

"Have mercy, O *Wakan-Tanka,* on the souls that have roamed the earth and have departed. May these souls be worthy to walk upon that great white path which You have established! We are about to light and smoke the sacred pipe, and we know that this offering is very *wakan.* The smoke that rises will spread throughout the universe, and all beings will rejoice."

The dancers then sat at the west side of the lodge, and the keeper took the tallow from the top of the bowl of the pipe and placed it upon a purified buffalo chip. The pipe was then lit from a coal, and, after offering it to the six directions, and after taking a few puffs himself, the keeper handed it to Kablaya, who cried as he offered the pipe and, after smoking it a little, handed it to the person next to him. After each man had offered and smoked the pipe, he handed it back to Kablaya, who then handed it on to the next man. When all had smoked in this manner, Kabalaya slowly and carefully placed the ashes upon the very middle of the sacred altar and then prayed.

"O *Wakan-Tanka,* this sacred place is Yours. Upon it all has been finished. We rejoice!"

Two helpers then placed upon the altar the ashes from the sacred fire at the east of the lodge; the purified earth was also placed upon the altar, and then all the wreaths, furs, feathers, and symbols which had been used in the dance were all piled up in the center of the sacred place. This was done because these things were too sacred to be kept and should be returned to the earth. Only the buffalo robes and the eagle-bone whistles were kept, and these things will always be regarded as especially sacred, for they were used in this first great rite of the sun dance. On top of the pile of sacred things the buffalo skull was placed, for this skull reminds us of death and also helps us to remember that a cycle has here been completed.

The people all rejoiced, and the little children were allowed to play tricks on the old people, at this time, but nobody cared; and they were not punished, for everybody was very happy.

The dancers, however, had not yet finished, for they now took their buffalo robes and returned to the preparation tipi. Here they took off their clothes, except for the breech cloth, and they all entered the *Inipi* lodge, except the woman who guarded the door for the men. The five rocks were brought in, and the pipe was smoked around the circle; but, as each man took the pipe, he first touched one of the rocks with it. The door of the lodge was closed, and Kablaya spoke.

"My relatives, I wish to say something. Listen closely! This day you have done a sacred thing, for you have given your bodies to the Great Spirit. When you return to your people always remember that through this act you have been made holy. In the future you will be the leaders of your people, and you should be worthy of this sacred duty. Be merciful to your people, be good to them and love them! But always remember this, that your closest relative is your Grandfather and your Father, *Wakan-Tanka,* and next to Him is your Grandmother and your Mother, the Earth."

Water was put on the hot rocks, and, after a short time, when the little lodge was filled with steam and was very hot, the door was opened and water was handed in. Sweet grass was put in the water and was then touched to the mouths of the dancers, but this was all the water that was allowed at this time. The pipe was passed around; the door was closed; and again Kablaya spoke to the men.

"By your actions today you have strengthened the sacred hoop of our nation. You have made a sacred center which will always be with you, and you have created a closer relationship with all things of the universe."

Water was again put on the rocks, and as the steam rose the men chanted a sacred song. When the door was opened this third time the men were allowed to drink one mouthful of water; after this the pipe was passed around as before. Again the door was closed, and as the steam rose from the rocks, all the men sang.

> *I am sending a voice to my Grandfather!*
> *I am sending a voice to my Grandfather!*
> *Hear me!*
> *Together with all things of the universe,*
> *I am sending a voice to* Wakan-Tanka.

Then Kablaya said: "The four paths of the four Powers are your close relatives. The dawn and the sun of the day are your relatives. The Morning Star and all the stars of the sacred heavens are your relatives; always remember this!"

The door was then opened for the fourth and last time, and the men drank all the water they wished; and when they had finished drinking and had smoked, Kablaya said to them: "You have now seen the Light of *Wakan-Tanka* four times. This Light will be with you always. Remember that it is four steps to the end of the sacred path.[5] But you shall get there. It is good! It is finished! *Hechetu welo!*"

The men then went back to the sacred tipi, where much food was brought to them, and all the people were happy and rejoicing, for a great thing had been done, and in the winters to come much strength would be given to the life of the nation through this great rite.

---

[5] The four steps represent, to the Sioux, the four ages or phases of a cycle: the rock age, the bow age, the fire age, and the pipe age. The rock, bow, fire, or pipe constitutes the main ritual support for each age. The four ages may also refer, microcosmically, to the four phases of a man's life, from birth to death.

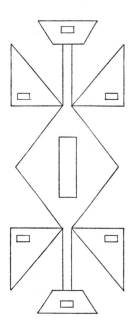

CHAPTER VI

Hunkapi: THE MAKING OF RELATIVES

In this rite we establish a relationship on earth, which is a reflection of that real relationship which always exists between man and *Wakan-Tanka*. As we always love *Wakan-Tanka* first, and before all else, so we should also love and establish closer relationships with our fellow men, even if they should be of another nation than ours. In establishing and participating in this rite which I shall describe, we are carrying out the will of the Great Spirit, for this is one of the seven rites which in the beginning the White Buffalo Cow Woman promised us.

Other nations claim that they were the originators of this rite, but this is not so, for it was the Lakota Matohoshila (Bear Boy), a very holy man, who received this rite in a vision from *Wakan-Tanka.*

You should know that the sacred plant, the corn, is not native to the Sioux, but long ago Matohoshila had his great vision about the corn, and then later, when traveling to the southeast, he found a small patch of the corn, exactly as he had seen in his vision; and this corn he brought back to his people, not knowing that it belonged to the Ree nation, with whom the Sioux had long been at war.[1]

Now corn was as important and sacred to the Ree as is the pipe to our people; therefore, shortly after their corn had disappeared, the Ree sent messengers to the camp of the Sioux, bearing many gifts and much of their twist tobacco which we prize highly, and asked for their corn back again.

The Sioux accepted the peace offering, and Matohoshila, who now understood the significance of his vision, told his people of it and said that by holding this rite now we shall establish a close and lasting relationship with the Ree nation—one that will endure until the end of time, and one that will be an example to all other nations.

All the people gladly accepted this and gave to Matohoshila the authority and power to establish the peace through the *hunkapi* rite. Matohoshila then explained that, whenever this rite is carried out, the one who wishes another to be his relative is regarded as a Ree, and it is he who must sing over the other. Matohoshila then told the visiting Ree to set up a sacred tipi and that they should choose one of their men to represent their whole Ree nation, and he should be the one to sing over Matohoshila, who in turn should represent the whole Sioux nation.

A little later, Matohoshila filled his pipe and went to the Ree who had been chosen to represent his people. Offering the pipe to him, Matohoshila said: "I wish you to help me in establishing a rite which, for the benefit of all our people, has been given to me in a vision by the Great Spirit. It is His will that we do this. He, who is our Grandfather and Father, has established a relationship with my people the Sioux; it is our duty to make a rite which should extend this relationship to the different people of different

[1] The Ree or Arikara are of the Caddo family and thus are closely related to the Pawnee.

nations. May that which we do here be an example to others!

"You represent the Ree people as a whole, and I represent the Sioux nation. You have come here in order to make peace, and we have accepted your offer; but, as you see, we are going to establish here something deeper than that for which you have asked. In asking for peace you have brought to us your tobacco which we cherish very much, and, likewise, we shall give to you the sacred corn which you cherish more than anything. They both are sacred, for they are from the Great Spirit; they have been made by Him for our use!"

Matohoshila then instructed the Ree how to make the offering which would later be brought to the Sioux and told him what equipment was necessary for the rite:

a pipe	dried buffalo meat
tobacco	red and dark blue paint
four stalks of corn with ears	eagle plumes
one cornstalk without ears	a knife
a buffalo skull	sweet grass
three sticks for a rack	dried buffalo bladder

When this equipment had been gathered, Matohoshila took a knife and made a clean place upon the earth inside the tipi. Upon this sacred place four live coals were placed, and upon them Matohoshila placed some sweet grass, and prayed.

"O Grandfather, *Wakan-Tanka,* behold us! Here we shall make relatives and peace; it is Your will that this be done. With this sweet grass which is Yours, I am now making smoke, which will rise to You. In everything that we do, You are first, and this our sacred Mother Earth is second, and next to Her are the four quarters. By making this rite we shall carry out Thy will upon this earth, and we shall make a peace that will last to the end of time. The smoke from this sweet grass will be upon everything in the universe. It is good!"

All the equipment was purified over the smoke; the three sticks were set up as a drying rack; and the pipe was rested against it. Matohoshila then put the buffalo bladder in front of him, and, holding up a piece of the tobacco to the west, he prayed.

"O You who guard the path where the sun goes down, and who control the waters! we are about to establish a relationship and a sacred peace. You have two sacred days—may the people have these, and may they walk the path of life with firm steps! You are to be included in this relationship and peace which we are about to establish; help us! We are making here on earth the same relationship which *Wakan-Tanka* always has with his people."

This tobacco which was identified with the Power of the west was then placed in the bladder.

I should perhaps tell you that the buffalo bladder is, for many peoples, as sacred as our pipe, for it also may contain the whole universe.

A pinch of tobacco was next offered to the north, with this prayer:

"O You where the giant Waziah lives, who control the purifying winds, You are to be placed in this sacred bag, and so help us with Your two holy days, and assist us in walking upon the straight path of life."

The Power of the north, now in the tobacco, was placed in the bag; and then Matohoshila offered a pinch of tobacco to the Power of the east.

"O You who control the path where the sun comes up, and who give knowledge, You are included in this offering, and so help us with Your two sacred days!"

After placing this Power of the east in the bag, a pinch of tobacco was offered, with a prayer, to the place where we always face.

"O You, White Swan, who control the path upon which the generations walk, there is a place for You in this sacred bag, and so help us with Your two red and blue days!"

After placing this Power of the south in the bag, Matohoshila offered a pinch of tobacco to the heavens.

"Grandfather, *Wakan-Tanka*, of the sacred heavens, Father, *Wakan-Tanka*, Grandmother Earth, and Mother Earth, may we know this our four-fold relationship with You; may we use this knowledge in making peace with another nation. By making relatives here on earth, we know that we do Thy will. O *Wakan-Tanka,* You are above everything, but You are here with us today."

This tobacco for the Great Spirit was then put into the bag, and, holding a pinch of tobacco to the ground, Matohoshila prayed.

"Grandmother Earth, hear me! Upon You we are making a relationship with a people, just as You have made a relationship with us, by bringing to us our sacred pipe. The two-leggeds, the four-leggeds, the wingeds, and all that move upon You are Your children. With all beings and all things we shall be as relatives; just as we are related to You, O Mother, so we shall make peace with another people and shall be related to them. May we walk with love and mercy upon that path which is holy! O Grandmother and Mother, we are placing You in this bag. Help us in making relatives and a lasting peace here!"

The Earth was then put in the bag, the mouth of which was tied, and the hair of a buffalo and some sweet grass were placed on top of it.

Matohoshila then said to the Ree: "You must now take care of this bag, which is very *wakan,* for it is really the same as the sacred pipe which was brought to us Sioux, and it, too, will make peace and relatives among many peoples. But you should always remember this, that our closest relatives are our Grandfather and Father, *Wakan-Tanka,* and our Grandmother and Mother, the Earth. With this sacred bag you should go to the leaders of the Sioux, and with it the relationship will be made."

The bag was then rolled up in a buckskin and tied at both ends with a rawhide rope in such a way that it could be carried easily. With this the first day of the rite was concluded.

The following day, just as the sun came up, Matohoshila took his pipe and went to the tipi of the Ree. After offering the pipe to the six directions, then smoking it a little, Matohoshila passed it to the Ree, who said, *"Hi ho! Hi ho!"* and embraced the pipe. After smoking for a few puffs, he passed it to the others in the tipi.

After the pipe had been passed among everybody, it was returned to Matohoshila, who then purified it and returned it to its bag. Then Matohoshila left for his own tipi, where he and the other Sioux chiefs and wise men were to wait for the Ree who was to come bearing the offering which he had been instructed to make the previous day.

When the Sioux saw the Ree approaching, they all cried *"Hi ho! Ho ho!"* and four of the Sioux went to meet him and led him into the tipi. The Ree walked around the lodge sun-wise, stood before Matohoshila, who was seated at the west, and placed before him the sacred offering bundle. A hot coal was placed before Matohoshila, who burned some sweet grass and held the sacred bundle over the smoke. Then after crying *"Hi ho! Hi ho!"* and embracing the bundle, he prayed.

"Grandfather, *Wakan-Tanka,* Father, *Wakan-Tanka,* behold us! Upon this earth we are fulfilling Thy will. By giving to us the sacred pipe, You have established a relationship with us, and this relationship we are now extending by making this peace with another nation with whom we were once at war. We know that we are now fulfilling one of the seven sacred rites which in the beginning were promised to us. Through this rite may these two peoples always live in peace, and set an example to other nations. With this offering my people will rejoice. This is a sacred day! It is good! Now we shall open this holy bundle, and through this offering we shall be bound to You and to all Your Powers. *Wakan-Tanka,* behold what we are doing!"

Matohoshila then slowly undid the *wakan* bundle, and when he and the people saw the buffalo bladder, they all cried *"Hi ye!"* for, of course, everybody knew why this bladder was so sacred. Matohoshila then held the bladder over the smoke of the sweet grass and embraced it, saying all the time, *"Hi ye!"* and then he prayed.

"Be merciful to me! Now that You have come to us, the people will walk the sacred path with their children in hand. I am the people, and I love You, shall cherish You, and shall always care for You. The people from whom You came [the Ree] will also always cherish You and will always know You to be *wakan.*"

Matohoshila then offered the bladder to the six directions, and, as he embraced it and kissed the opening of the bag, all the people cried *"Hi ho!"* Then, turning to the Ree, Matohoshila said: "To our people this offering means that you wish peace, and that you wish to establish a relationship with us. Is it for this reason that you have brought such a sacred offering?"

"Yes!" the Ree replied, "we wish to have a relationship with you which is as close as the relationship which exists between your people and *Wakan-Tanka.*"

The Sioux were pleased at this reply, and the sacred bladder was then sent out of the lodge and was passed around among all the people, who embraced it and kissed its mouth, in the same manner that Matohoshila had done. In order now to show that the peace offering of the Ree had been accepted, and in order to place the bundle at the very most sacred place, it was tied at the top of the twenty-eighth lodge pole. As I have explained before, this twenty-eighth pole represents *Wakan-Tanka,* for it is this key pole which holds up all the twenty-seven other poles of the tipi. In this manner the bringing of the offering was finished, and then the Ree returned to their lodges in order to prepare for the next day; Matohoshila, too, prepared a special tipi for the rites which were to come. This special lodge had, at either side of the entrance, hides which formed a pathway some ten strides long and about four feet high, and this makes the road of life leading into the tipi; thus, you see that one who enters upon this path cannot turn either to the right or left because of this screen of hides; he must walk straight to the center.

The following day four Ree were chosen to represent the whole nation, and bearing with them the equipment needed for the rites of the day, they went to the lodge which Matohoshila had prepared. Within the lodge Matohoshila was seated at the west and was preparing to make the sacred altar, but first he spoke, saying: "The corn that we Sioux now have really belongs to the Ree, for they cherish it and regard it as sacred, in the same manner that we regard our pipe; for they, too, have received their corn through a vision from the Great Spirit. It is the will of *Wakan-Tanka* that they have their corn. Thus, we shall not only return to them their lost corn but we shall also at this time establish a rite in which we shall create not only peace but also a real relationship which will be a reflection of that relationship which exists between us and *Wakan-Tanka*.

"I will now make a fragrant smoke which will reach to the sacred heavens and to the morning star, which divides the day into darkness and light, and it will reach, also, to the four Powers which guard the universe. This smoke is now going forth from our Grandmother and Mother Earth."

Matohoshila then put sweet grass upon the coals, and over the smoke he purified the sacred pipe, the corn, the hatchet, and all the equipment; he was now ready to make the sacred altar.

Taking up the hatchet, Matohoshila pointed it to the six directions and then struck the ground at the west. Again pointing the hatchet to the six directions, he struck the ground at the north, and in the same manner the other two directions were established. Then holding the hatchet to the heavens, he struck the ground twice at the center for the Earth and then again twice at the center for the Great Spirit. He scraped the ground level, and with a stick which had been purified, and which was first offered to the six directions, he drew a line from the west to the center, and then from the east to the center, from the north to the center, from the south to the center, and then, offering the stick to the heavens, he touched the center, and offering the stick to the earth, he again touched the center. In this manner the altar was made, and, as I have said before, it is very sacred, for we have here established the center of the Earth, and this center, which in reality is everywhere, is the home, the dwelling place of *Wakan-Tanka*.

Matohoshila took up an ear of corn, and at one end of it he pushed in a stick, and at the other end of the ear he tied the plume of an eagle.

"This corn really belongs to the Ree," Matohoshila said, "and so it will be returned to them, because they cherish it as we do our pipe. The ear of the corn which you see here has twelve important meanings connected with it, for there are twelve rows of kernels, which it receives from the various powers of the universe. As we think of the different things the corn can teach us, we should, above all, never forget the peace and the relationship which it is establishing here. But always, above everything else, we should remember that our closest relatives are our Grandfather and Father, *Wakan-Tanka,* our Grandmother and Mother, the Earth, the four Powers of the universe, the red and blue days, the two divisions of the day [light and darkness], the morning star, the Spotted Eagle, who guards all that is sacred about the corn; and also our pipe, which is as a relative, for he guards the people; and it is through him that we pray to *Wakan-Tanka.*

"The tassel which grows upon the top of the ear of corn, and which we have represented here by the eagle plume, represents the presence of the Great Spirit, for, as the pollen from the tassel spreads all over, giving life, so it is with *Wakan-Tanka,* who gives life to all things. This plume, which is always on top of the plant, is the first to see the light of the dawn as it comes, and it sees also the night and the moon and all the stars. For all these reasons it is very *wakan.* And this stick which I have stuck into the ear of corn is the tree of life, reaching from Earth to Heaven, and the fruit, which is the ear with all its kernels, represents the people and all things of the universe. It is good to remember these things if we are to understand the rites which are to come."

Matohoshila then rested the ear of corn against the rack which had been set up near the sacred altar; this rack was an image of the rack upon which the buffalo meat was dried, and it was now a drying rack for corn, for, you see, the corn was as important to the Ree as was the buffalo to the Sioux.

Matohoshila took off an ear of corn from its stalk, and giving it to the Ree, said: "It is the will of *Wakan-Tanka* that this corn return to you. In this way we shall make peace and establish a relationship which shall be an example to all nations. We have often spoken of the twelve Powers of the universe; we shall bind these twelve Powers, with the Sioux and the Ree, into one. In doing this, the Ree must sing over the Sioux. I shall represent my people; your chief shall represent your nation; and, by our becoming related, these two nations will be as one and shall live in peace. In the past, the two-leggeds which *Wakan-Tanka* placed upon this island have been enemies, but through this rite there will be peace, and, in the future, through this rite other nations of this island will become as relatives.

"You Ree should now pretend that you are on the warpath with us; you should go out and scout for the enemy, singing your war songs."

Holding ears of the corn in their right hands and cornstalks in their left hands, the Ree then pretended that they were scouting for the enemy—the Sioux. As they chanted their war songs, they waved the cornstalks back and forth. The swinging of the cornstalks in this manner is very *wakan*, for it represents the corn when the breath of the Great Spirit is upon it, since, when the wind blows, the pollen drops from the tassel upon the silk surrounding the ear, through which the fruit becomes mature and fertile.

You thus see that this relationship illustrated by the example of the corn is the same as that which we are establishing between these two peoples.

As the Ree pretended to be scouting for their enemy, the Sioux, all the people gathered about to watch them, and everybody was really very happy, for they understood that which was being done here. Soon the Ree stood in front of the tipi within which were the four Sioux; the Ree chief addressed his braves.

"Which of you has been the first to make a coup on the warpath? It is for you now to count coup on this lodge and then to go in and capture Matohoshila; and afterwards we shall capture the rest. But first you must tell us of your great deeds done on the warpath."

The chosen Ree then began to tell of his brave deeds, and, after each sentence, the people all cried *"Hi ho! Hi ho!"* and the women gave the tremulo. When he had finished, the Ree rushed at the tipi, counting coup; and then they entered and brought out Matohoshila. The other Ree captured and brought out the other four Sioux. The Ree continued to chant their war songs, and all the people—Ree and Sioux—were very happy and gave each other gifts of food, clothing, and even horses.

Then a procession was formed, led by the Ree who were still swinging the cornstalks, and after them came the five captured Sioux, among whom there was a Lakota woman and a small boy and a girl, for in all these people the whole nation was represented. The children were carried on the shoulders of the Ree, and at the end of the procession came the singers, drummers, and all the people of both nations who were watching. The procession stopped four times, and each time they stopped they howled as do the coyotes, for this is what is always done by a returning war party. Soon they came to the sacred lodge which had been prepared at the center of the camping circle, and the captured Sioux were led to beds at the west of the lodge, upon which were piled many gifts which the Ree were really giving to the Sioux.

The Ree helpers then took buffalo robes and held them up in front of the five Sioux and the Ree chief, and this is called "the hiding of the *hunkas*." A Ree warrior and a Ree woman then went behind the curtain and began to paint the faces of the Sioux. The woman painted the faces of the Sioux woman and the Sioux girl red, and the Ree warrior painted the faces of the Lakota men and the boy red, with a blue circle around the face, and a blue line on the forehead, on both cheek bones, and on the chin. And all the time that the people were being painted, the Ree were still swinging the cornstalks, and were chanting their sacred song. The eagle plumes were then taken off the ears of corn and were put in the hair of the Sioux. While all this was being done, a buffalo skull was painted red, and the four Powers were represented by four lines upon it; sage was stuffed in the eyes and nose of the skull, and it was then placed—facing east—on a mound of earth which had been scraped from the sacred place.

The buffalo robes were then taken aside so that all could see the Sioux who had been painted. I should perhaps explain here what this represents. By being painted, the people have been changed; they have undergone a new birth, and with this they have new responsibilities, new obligations, and a new relationship. This transformation is so sacred that it must be undergone in darkness; it must be hidden from the view of the people. But when the curtain is taken aside, they come forth pure, free from ignorance, and must now have forgotten all troubles of the past. They are now one with the Ree; the relationship has been made.

Swinging their cornstalks, the Rees then chanted.

> *All these are related* [hunka].
> *All these are relatives.*

Then turning to each of the four directions, they chanted:

> *O You, Power, there where the sun goes down:*
> *You are a relative.*
> *O You, Power, where the Giant lives:*
> *You are a relative.*
> *O You, where the sun comes from:*
> *You are a relative.*
> *O You, Power, there where we always face:*
> *You are a relative.*

And then looking towards the Heaven, they chanted:

> *That relative!*

And bending over the Earth, and also over the buffalo, they chanted:

> *The Earth is our relative.*

And finally, waving the corn over the five Sioux, they chanted:

> *These four are our relatives;*
> *We are all related;*
> *We are all one!*

Matohoshila then rose, and, taking the pipe from the rack, he stood in the middle of the tipi, and, raising his right hand, and holding up the pipe in his left hand, he prayed.

"O *Wakan-Tanka,* I raise my hand to You. This day You are standing close to us. I offer You my pipe. To You also, O winged Power where the sun goes down, we offer this pipe. On this holy day, we have united into one all that is sacred in the universe. On this day a true relationship has been established. On this day a great peace has been made. O Grandfather, *Wakan-Tanka,* Your will which You have taught us has been done here on this earth. May this peace and relationship always be, and may no person or circumstance ever destroy it. It is now about to be completed; there will be peace, and these peoples will walk together that one path which is red and sacred."

Turning then to the people, Matohoshila said: "Now it is nearly finished, for we are bound together; we are one! O you Ree, that corn which you cherished, but lost, will be given back to you!"

At this all the people cheered loudly, and the women gave the tremulo. Once again the chanting began, and the two Ree with the cornstalks danced towards the door at the east, and then five times they rushed towards the five Sioux, and after this the swinging and dancing ceased.

Much food was brought into the tipi, and, purifying pieces of dried buffalo meat over the smoke of sweet grass, the Ree chief said: "O *Wakan-Tanka,* behold me and be merciful to me! This meat is the *hoksi chan ki ya* [root or seed]; it is to be placed in Your mouth, and it will become Your body and soul, which the Great Spirit has given to You with all His goodness. As He is merciful to You, so You too must be merciful to others!"

This the Ree chief said, as he put the sacred meat in the mouth of each of the four Sioux; and then he and Matohoshila moved and sat opposite each other at the center of the tipi. In front of Matohoshila was the buffalo skull and the pipe, and in front of the Ree chief there was the ear of corn and the four cornstalks. The Ree chief then took up a piece of the buffalo meat, and, after purifying it in the smoke of sweet grass, he held it in front of Matohoshila.

"*Ho,* son! I am to be your father. On this day which belongs to *Wakan-Tanka* He has seen our faces; the dawn of this day has seen us, and our Grandmother, the Earth, has listened to us. We are here at the center, and the four Powers of the universe join in us. This meat I shall put in your mouth, and from this day forth you shall never fear my home, for my home is your home, and you are my son!"

The chief then put the meat in Matohoshila's mouth, and at this all the Ree people rejoiced and gave thanks, for by this act the two people had been made one. Then Matohoshila, in turn, took up a piece of meat, purified it over the smoke, and, holding it in front of the Ree chief, said:

"*Ho,* Father! This day we have done the will of the Great Spirit, and through this we have established a relationship and peace, not only among ourselves, but within ourselves and with all the Powers of the universe. The dawn of the day has surely seen us, and with us today there has been the buffalo, who is our source of life here on earth, and who guards the people; and there has been with us our sacred pipe, which gives to our people the food for their souls; and also we have had with us your corn, which is so sacred to you, and with which we have made peace and have created a relationship. This food I shall place in your mouth, so you will never fear my home, for it is your home. In doing this, may *Wakan-Tanka* be merciful to us."

Matohoshila then placed the meat in the mouth of the Ree chief, and for this act all the Sioux cheered and gave thanks. Then, taking up his pipe and lighting it, Matohoshila offered it to the six directions and, after puffing on it four times, handed it to the Ree, saying: "*Ho,* father! Take this and smoke it with nothing but the truth in your heart."

The Ree took the sacred pipe, offered it to the six directions, and, after puffing on it four times, handed it around among the people. All the Ree and Sioux then took turns smoking it, and even after the fire had gone out, they put it to their mouths and embraced it. As the pipe was being passed among the people, the Ree chief said to Matohoshila:

"*Ho,* son! You have given back to us the corn which *Wakan-Tanka* had given to us, but which you took from us because of a vision which you had. Since we wanted our corn back, we came to you offering peace; but you have given to us more than this by making this relationship here today. In order now to bind us even more closely together, I give back to you a part of the corn and the freedom to use it in your rites. You, too, may now regard it as sacred as we do."

All the people were very happy that this great thing had been done, and they then held a feast which lasted throughout the night.

I wish to mention here, that through these rites a three-fold peace was established. The first peace, which is the most important, is that which comes within the souls of men when they realize their relationship, their oneness, with the universe and all its Powers, and when they realize that at the center of the universe dwells *Wakan-Tanka,* and that this center is really everywhere, it is within each of us. This is the real Peace, and the others are but reflections of this. The second peace is that which is made between two individuals, and the third is that which is made between two nations. But above all you should understand that there can never be peace between nations until there is first known that true peace which, as I have often said, is within the souls of men.

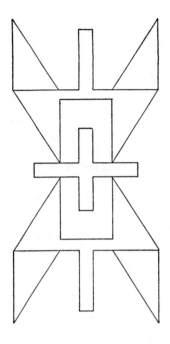

CHAPTER VII

Ishna Ta Awi Cha Lowan:
PREPARING A GIRL FOR WOMANHOOD

These rites are performed after the first menstrual period of a woman. They are important because it is at this time that a young girl becomes a woman, and she must understand the meaning of this change and must be instructed in the duties which she is now to fulfill. She should realize that the change which has taken place in her is a sacred thing, for now she will be as Mother Earth and will be able to bear children, which should also be brought up in a sacred manner. She should know, further, that each month when her period arrives she bears an influence with which she must be careful, for the presence of a woman in this condition may take away the power of a holy man. Thus, she should observe carefully the rites of purification which we shall describe here, for these rites were given to us by *Wakan-Tanka* through a vision.

Ishna Ta Awi Cha Lowan: PREPARING FOR WOMANHOOD

Before we received these rites[1] it was customary that during each menstrual period the woman or young girl should go to a small tipi apart from the camping circle; food was brought to her, and no one else could go near the tipi. During the first period of a young girl, she was instructed by an older woman in the things a woman should know, even in the making of moccasins and clothes. This older woman who helped the girl should have been a good and holy person, for at this time her virtues and habits passed into the young girl whom she was purifying. Before she was permitted to return to her family and to her people the young girl had to be further purified in the *Inipi* lodge. But now I shall tell you how we received the new rites for preparing our young girls for womanhood.

A Lakota by the name of Slow Buffalo (*Tatanka Hunkeshne*) once had a vision of a buffalo calf who was being cleansed by her mother, and through the power of this vision Slow Buffalo became a holy man (*wichasha wakan*) and understood that he had been given rites which should be used for the benefit of the young women of his nation.

A few moons after Slow Buffalo received his vision, a young girl of fourteen called "White Buffalo Cow Woman Appears," had her first period, and of course her father, Feather on Head, thought immediately of Slow Buffalo's vision, so he took a filled pipe and offered it to Slow Buffalo, who accepted it, saying: *"Hi ho! Hi ho!* For what reason do you bring this sacred pipe?"

"I have a girl who is about to pass through her first period," Feather on Head replied, "and I want you to purify her and prepare her for womanhood, for I know that you have had a very powerful vision through which you have learned how this should be done in a better and more *wakan* manner than that which we have followed."

"Certainly, I shall do as you wish," Slow Buffalo replied. "The buffalo people, who have been taught by *Wakan-Tanka,* and who have given us this rite, are next to the two-leggeds, and are our source of life in many ways. For it was the White Buffalo Cow

[1] *Ishna Ta Awi Cha Lowan* is literally "Her alone they sing over."

117

Woman who, in the beginning, brought to us our most sacred pipe, and from that time we have been relatives with the four-leggeds and all that moves. *Tatanka,* the buffalo, is the closest four-legged relative that we have, and they live as a people, as we do. It is the will of our Grandfather, *Wakan-Tanka,* that this be so; it is His will that this rite be done here on earth by the two-leggeds. We shall now establish a sacred rite that will be of great benefit to all the people. It is true that all the four-leggeds and all the peoples who move on the universe have this rite of purification, and especially our relative the buffalo, for, as I have seen, they too purify their children and prepare them for bearing fruit. It will be a sacred day when we do this, and it will please *Wakan-Tanka* and all the peoples who move. All these peoples, and all the Powers of the universe, you must first place in the pipe, so that with them we may send a voice to the Great Spirit!

"I shall make a sacred place for your daughter, who is pure, and who is about to become a woman. The dawn of the day, which is the Light of *Wakan-Tanka,* will be upon this place, and all will be sacred.

"Tomorrow you must build a tipi just outside of the camping circle, and it must be built with a sheltered way leading to it, as is done in the *hunkapi* rite, and then you must gather together the following things:

a buffalo skull	a pipe
a wooden cup	some Ree tobacco
some cherries	*kinnikinnik*
water	a knife
sweet grass	a stone hatchet
sage	some red and blue paint

Feather on Head then gave to Slow Buffalo offerings of horses, and other gifts, and then he left to prepare for the next day.

The following day everything had been made ready in the sacred tipi, and all the people gathered around it, except those women who were preparing the feast which would come after the rites. Slow Buffalo was seated at the west of the tipi, and in front of him a place had been scraped in the earth, where a hot coal was placed. Holding sweet grass above the coal, Slow Buffalo prayed.

"Grandfather, *Wakan-Tanka,* Father, *Wakan-Tanka,* I offer to You Your sacred herb. O Grandmother Earth, from whence we come, and Mother Earth, who bears much fruit, listen! I am going to make smoke which will penetrate the heavens, reaching even to our Grandfather, *Wakan-Tanka;* it will spread over the whole universe, touching all things!"

After placing the sweet grass on the coal, Slow Buffalo purified first the pipe and then all the equipment which was to be used in the rite.

"All that will be done today," Slow Buffalo said, "will be accomplished with the aid of the Powers of the universe. May they help us to purify and to make sacred this girl who is about to become a woman. I now fill this sacred pipe, and in doing this I am placing within it all the Powers, who are helping us here today!"

Slow Buffalo first purified himself over the smoke, and then, holding the pipe in his left hand, he took a pinch of tobacco and prayed.

"Grandfather, *Wakan-Tanka,* we are about to send a voice through our pipe to You. This is a special day, for we are about to purify this young girl, White Buffalo Cow Woman Appears. There is a place for all the Powers of the universe in this pipe, and so have mercy upon us and accept our offering!

"O You where the sun goes down, who guard the pipe, and who come so terribly in order to purify the world and its people, we are about to offer this pipe to *Wakan-Tanka* and need Your help today, especially with your cleansing waters, for we are about to purify and make sacred not only a young girl, but also a whole generation. Help us with your two good red and blue days! There is a place for you in the pipe!"

Slow Buffalo put this tobacco in the pipe, and then, holding some tobacco to the place from which come the purifying winds (the north), he prayed.

"O You, giant *Waziah,* Power of the north, who guard the

health of the people with your winds, and who purify the earth by making it white, you are the one who watches that path upon which our people walk. Help us especially today with your purifying influence, for we are about to make sacred a virgin, White Buffalo Cow Woman Appears, from whom will come the generations of our people. There is a place for you in this pipe, help us with your two good days!"

The power of the north was put in the pipe, and then, holding a pinch of tobacco to the direction from which the light comes, Slow Buffalo continued to pray.

"O You, *Huntka,* the being and power of that place from whence comes the dawn of the day and the light of *Wakan-Tanka;* O You who are long-winded, and who give knowledge to the people, give of Your wisdom today to this virgin, White Buffalo Cow Woman Appears, who is about to be purified. Help us with Your two red and blue days. There is a place for You in the pipe."

Slow Buffalo then put into the pipe this Power of the place from whence comes the light, and then, holding tobacco to the place towards which we always face (the south), he prayed.

"O You, White Swan, Power of the place where we always face, who control the path of the generations and of all that moves, we are about to purify a virgin, that her generations to come may walk in a sacred manner upon that path which You control. There is a place for You in the pipe! Help us with Your two red and blue days!"

The Power of the south was then put in the pipe, and, holding now a pinch of tobacco up to the heavens, Slow Buffalo continued.

"O *Wakan-Tanka,* Grandfather, behold us! We are about to offer the pipe to You!" [Then holding the tobacco to the earth]:

"O You, Grandmother, upon whom the generations of the people have walked, may White Buffalo Cow Woman Appears and her generations walk upon you in a sacred manner in the winters to come. O Mother Earth, who gives forth fruit, and who is as a mother to the generations, this young virgin who is here today will be purified and made sacred; may she be like You, and may her children and her children's children walk the sacred path in a holy manner. Help us, O Grandmother and Mother, with Your red and blue days!"

The Earth, as Grandmother and Mother, was now in the tobacco, and was placed in the pipe, and again Slow Buffalo held tobacco towards the heavens and prayed.

"O *Wakan-Tanka,* behold us! We are about to offer this pipe to You." [Then pointing the same tobacco to the buffalo skull]: "O you, our four-legged relative, and who of all the four-legged peoples are the nearest to the two-leggeds, you too are to be placed in the pipe, for you have taught us how you cleanse your young, and it is this your way that we shall use in purifying White Buffalo Cow Woman Appears. I give to you as an offering, O four-legged, water, paint, cherry juice, and also grass. There is a place for you in the pipe—help us!"

Thus all the four-legged buffalo people were placed in the pipe, and now for the last time Slow Buffalo held tobacco up to *Wakan-Tanka* and prayed.

"O *Wakan-Tanka* and all the winged Powers of the universe, behold us! This tobacco I offer especially to You, the Chief of all the Powers, who is represented by the Spotted Eagle who lives in the depths of the heavens, and who guards all that is there! We are about to purify a young girl, who is soon to be a woman. May You guard those generations which will come forth from her! There is a place for You in the pipe—help us with the red and blue days!"

The pipe, containing now the whole universe, was leaned against the little drying rack, with its "foot" on the earth, and its "mouth" pointing towards the heavens. Then Slow Buffalo prepared to make the sacred place, and only the close relatives of White Buffalo Cow Woman Appears were allowed within the tipi, for the rites which were to follow are too sacred to be seen by all the people.

"*Wakan-Tanka* has given to the people a fourfold relationship—with their Grandfather, Father, Grandmother, and Mother," Slow Buffalo said. "These are always our closest relatives. Since all that is good is done in fours, the two-leggeds will walk through four ages, being relatives with all things. Our closest relative among the four-leggeds is *tatanka,* the buffalo, and I wish to tell you that they have established a relationship with me. I am about to make a sacred place for this virgin, White Buffalo Cow Woman Appears, and I have been given the power to do this from the buffalo. All things and all beings have been gathered together here today to witness this and to help us. It is so! *Hechetu welo!"*

Smoke was then made from the sweet grass, and, standing over it, Slow Buffalo again purified his whole body. When this was finished it was necessary before making the sacred place that Slow Buffalo demonstrate to all the people that he had truly received a power from the buffalo; so he began to chant his holy song which the buffalo had taught him.

> *This they are coming to see!*
> *I am going to make a place which is sacred.*
> *That they are coming to see.*
> *White Buffalo Cow Woman Appears*
> *Is sitting in a* wakan *manner.*
> *They are all coming to see her!*

Just then, as Slow Buffalo finished this song, he let out a loud *Huh!* like the bellow of a buffalo. As he did this a red dust came out of his mouth, just as a buffalo cow is able to do when she has a calf. This Slow Buffalo did six times, blowing the red smoke on the girl, and on the sacred place; everywhere within the tipi there was nothing but this red smoke, and if there were any children peeping in the door of the tipi, they were frightened and ran quickly away, for it was indeed a very terrible sight.

Slow Buffalo then took up his stone hatchet, and after purifying it over the smoke of the sweet grass, he struck the ground near the center of the tipi and then began to dig out a hollow in the shape of a buffalo wallow, piling the loose earth in a little mound just to the east of this sacred place. He then took a pinch of tobacco and, after holding it up to the heavens, placed it at the center of this place; then with tobacco he made a line from the west to the east and another line from the north to the south, thus making a cross. The whole universe was now within this holy place. Then taking some of the blue paint, and after holding it up to the heavens, Slow Buffalo touched the center of the sacred place. With more paint he drew blue lines on top of the tobacco, first from the west to the east, and then from the north to the south.

The use of this blue paint is very important and very sacred, if you understand the meaning, for, as I have often said, the power of a thing or an act is in the understanding of its meaning. Blue is the color of the heavens, and by placing the blue upon the tobacco, which represents the earth, we have united heaven and earth, and all has been made one.

Slow Buffalo then placed a buffalo skull upon the earth mound, with its face towards the east; then he painted a red line around its head and a straight red line between the horns, running down the forehead. Next he put balls of sage in the eyes of the skull, and then placed a wooden bowl of water in front of the buffalo's mouth. Cherries were placed in the water, for these represent the fruits of the earth, which are the same as the fruits of the two-leggeds. The cherry tree you see is the universe, and it stretches from Earth to Heaven; the fruits which the tree bears, and which are red as are we two-leggeds, are as all the fruits of our Mother, the Earth; for this and for more reasons than I could tell, this tree is very sacred to us.

Slow Buffalo next made a little bundle with sweet grass, the bark of the cherry tree, and the hair of a live buffalo. This hair is very *wakan* because it has been taken off a living tree, for you see the buffalo people, too, have a religion, and this is their offering which they have made to the tree.

White Buffalo Cow Woman Appears was then told to stand, and, holding this bundle of sacred things over her head, Slow Buffalo said:

"This which is over your head is like *Wakan-Tanka,* for when you stand you reach from Earth to Heaven; thus, anything above your head is like the Great Spirit. You are the tree of life. You will now be pure and holy, and may your generations to come be fruitful! Wherever your feet touch will be a sacred place, for now you will always carry with you a very great influence. May the four Powers of the universe help to purify you, for, as I mention the name of each power, I shall rub this bundle down that side of you. May the cleansing waters from where the sun goes down purify you! May you be as the purifying snow which comes from the place where *Waziah* lives. When the dawn of the day comes upon you, may you receive knowledge from the morning star. May you be made pure by the Power of the place towards which we always face, and may those peoples who have walked this straight and good path help to purify you. May you be as the White Swan who lives at this place there where you face, and may your children be as pure as the children of the Swan!"

The young girl sat down, and Slow Buffalo began to explain to the people how he had received his power from the buffalo, in a vision.

"I saw a great people who were breaking camp in preparation for a journey. I went towards them, and then suddenly they all gathered in a circle, and I was there with them. Then they brought a child into the center, and they told me that this child was to be purified according to the custom of their people. They then made a sacred place, a buffalo wallow as we have made here, and upon it they placed the child and asked me to breathe upon her, that she might be purified. I breathed upon her, but soon they said to me that they would show me their way which is better, and immediately they all turned into buffalo, and then a large bull came and blew a red powder upon the little calf in the center. As the calf lay there all the buffalo came and licked her, and each time they licked her they snorted and a sacred red smoke came out of their noses and mouths. They told me that this was the way that they purified their children. Now that the little buffalo calf had been purified, she would go forth and would bear fruit in a sacred manner, and in going forth she would travel to the end of the four ages; she would walk the sacred path as a leader of her people, and she would teach her children, too, to walk the path of life in a sacred manner. After showing me this they then established a

Seven Sioux Warriors who participated in the battle of the Little Big
Horn: left to right, *top row*: Iron Hail, age 90; High Eagle, age 88; Iron
Hawk, age 99; Little Warrior, age 80; *bottom row*: Comes Again, age
86; Pemmican, age 85; John Sitting Bull, age 80 *(Illuminated Foto-Ad
Service, Sioux Falls, S. D.)*

relationship with me, for they showed me a large buffalo bull and said that He would be my Grandfather, and then showing me a younger buffalo they said that He would be my Father; then they pointed to a buffalo cow and said that She was my Grandmother, and finally showing me a younger cow they said that She would be my Mother. They said that, with this fourfold relationship, I should return to my people and that I should teach them what I had been taught there. This is what I saw, and this is what I am doing here in purifying one of my own people in this manner; for this virgin, White Buffalo Cow Woman Appears, is that little calf which I saw. I shall now take her to drink of the sacred water, and this water is Life."

Slow Buffalo then began to sing another of his holy songs.

> *These peoples are sacred;*
> *From all over the universe they are coming to see it.*
> *White Buffalo Cow Woman Appears is sitting here in*
> * a sacred manner;*
> *They are all coming to see her.*

Slow Buffalo then picked up the buffalo skull by the horns, and, as he chanted his holy song, red smoke came out of the nose of the buffalo skull. Acting as a buffalo would, he began to push the young girl with the skull, shoving her towards the bowl of water, at which she then knelt and drank four sips; and when all the people saw all this it made them very happy.

A piece of buffalo meat was then given to Slow Buffalo; after purifying it over the smoke of the sweet grass, and after offering it to the six directions, he held it in front of the girl and said:

"White Buffalo Cow Woman Appears, you have prayed to *Wakan-Tanka;* you will now go forth among your people in a holy manner, and you will be an example to them. You will cherish those things which are most sacred in the universe; you will be as Mother Earth—humble and fruitful. May your steps, and those of your children, be firm and sacred! As *Wakan-Tanka* has been merciful to you, so you, too, must be merciful to others, especially to those children who are without parents. If such a child should ever come to your lodge, and if you should have but one piece of meat which you have already placed in your mouth, you should take it out and give it to her. You should be as generous as this! As I now place this meat in your mouth, we should all remember how merciful *Wakan-Tanka* is in providing for our wants. In the same manner you must provide for your children!"

Slow Buffalo placed the meat in the mouth of the girl, and then the bowl of water with the cherries was passed around among all the people, and each took a sip from it. Then Slow Buffalo took up the pipe from its rack, and, holding the stem up, he prayed.

"*Hee-ay-hay-ee-ee!* [four times] Grandfather, *Wakan-Tanka,* behold them! These people and all the generations to come are Yours. Look upon this virgin, White Buffalo Cow Woman Appears, who has been purified and honored this good day. May Your Light which never fails be upon her always and upon all her relatives! Grandmother, and great Mother Earth, upon You the people will walk; may they follow the sacred path with Light, not with the darkness of ignorance. May they always remember their relatives at the four quarters, and may they know that they are related to all that moves upon the universe, and especially the buffalo, who is the chief of the four-leggeds, and who helps to raise the people. O *Wakan-Tanka,* help us and be merciful to us, that we may live in a happy and sacred manner. Be merciful to us, *Wakan-Tanka,* that we may live!"

All the people then said "*Hi ho! Hi ho!*" and everybody was rejoicing and happy because of the great thing which had been done that day. White Buffalo Cow Woman Appears was brought out of the tipi, and all the people rushed up to her and placed their hands upon her, for now she was a woman, and, because of the rites which had been performed for her, there was much holiness in her. There was then a great feast, and a "give away," and those who were poor received much. It was in this manner that the rites for preparing a young girl for womanhood were first begun, and they have been the source of much holiness, not only for our women, but for the whole nation.

CHAPTER VIII

Tapa Wanka Yap: THE THROWING OF THE BALL

There was, until recently, a game among our people which was played with a ball, four teams and four goals which were set up at the four quarters. But there are only a few of us today who still understand why the game is sacred, or what the game originally was long ago, when it was not really a game, but one of our most important rites. This rite I am going to describe now, for it is the seventh and last sacred rite of this period given to us, through a vision, by *Wakan-Tanka.*

The game as it is played today represents the course of a man's life, which should be spent in trying to get the ball, for the ball represents *Wakan-Tanka,* or the universe, as I shall explain later. In the game today it is very difficult to get the ball, for the odds— which represent ignorance—are against you, and it is only one or two of the teams who are able to get the ball and score with it. But

127

in the original rite everybody was able to have the ball, and if you think about what the ball represents, you will see that there is much truth in it.

It was a Lakota called *Waskn mani* (Moves Walking), who received this rite in a vision many winters ago. He did not tell anybody about it for a very long time, until one day a Lakota called High Hollow Horn saw in a dream that Moves Walking had received a sacred rite which should belong to all the people. Thus, according to our custom, High Hollow Horn made a sacred tipi on one side of the camping circle; he then filled his pipe in a ritual manner, and with four other holy men, he went and offered the pipe to Moves Walking.

"*Hi ho! Hi ho! Hechetu welo,* it is good!" Moves Walking said, "What is it that you wish of me?"

"I have been told through a dream," High Hollow Horn said, "that you have received a very sacred rite which will be the seventh rite which the White Buffalo Cow Woman promised us in the beginning. All the people wish you to perform this rite now!"

"It is so," Moves Walking replied. "Announce to all the people that tomorow will be a holy day and that they must all paint their faces and wear their finest clothes. We will have this rite which *Wakan-Tanka* has sent to me through the buffalo!"

Moves Walking then held the pipe to heaven and prayed: "O Grandfather, *Wakan-Tanka,* behold us! You have given to us this pipe, that we may come closer to You. With the pipe we have walked upon the sacred path through this age. We have done Thy will here on earth, and now we will once again offer this pipe to You. Give to us a holy red and blue day! May it be sacred; may all rejoice!"

Moves Walking then told High Hollow Horn and the four other holy men that they should gather together the following things:

a pipe	a ball—made of buffalo hair,
some *kinnikinnik*	and covered with buffalo
sweet grass	skin

a Spotted Eagle feather   a bag of earth
a knife   some red and blue paint
a hatchet   a buffalo skull
some sage   a food rack, painted blue

The five men then left to prepare for the following day, and by now very many people had gathered around the sacred lodge, for they could see that something important was soon to happen. One man said that "this must be the seventh rite, for until now we have had only six, and I believe it will be a game which will represent life. I think they will throw a ball, for I just heard that it is to be a part of the equipment. Tomorrow should be a great day!" All that night the people talked about what was to happen the next day, and everybody was happy, for that which the White Buffalo Cow Woman had promised would now be fulfilled.

Before dawn the next day, all had been prepared, and the floor of the sacred lodge had been strewn with sage. Just before the sun came up, Moves Walking slowly approached the tipi, crying as he walked, for he had been thinking of the six other rites that his people had, and he knew that today the White Buffalo Cow Woman would again be with them. Many people went out to meet Moves Walking, and they also cried as they approached the sacred tipi; Moves Walking entered first, and after sitting at the place where the sun goes down, he cleared a place in front of him with a knife and then asked the helpers to bring a coal from the fire. He took sweet grass, and holding it over the coal, he prayed.

"Grandfather, *Wakan-Tanka,* You have always been and always shall be. You have created everything—there is nothing which does not belong to You. You have brought the red people to this island, and You have given us knowledge that we may know all things. We know that it is Your light which comes with the dawn, and we know that it is the Morning Star who gives us wisdom. You have given us the power to know the four Beings of the universe and to know that these four are really One. We see always the sacred heavens, and we know what they are and what they represent. This day will be a great day, and all that moves upon the earth and in the universe will rejoice. On this day I put Your sweet grass upon the fire which is also Yours, and the smoke which goes forth will spread throughout the universe and will reach even to the depths of the heavens."

Moves Walking brought the sweet grass down on the coal, stopping four times; then he purified the pipe, the ball, the buffalo skull, and all the equipment which was to be used that day.

"O *Wakan-Tanka,* my Grandfather," Moves Walking prayed, "I have used Your sweet grass, and the smoke has spread throughout the universe. Here I will build the sacred place, and the day which is now approaching will see it. They will look at each other face to face. In doing this I am fulfilling Your will. This is Your place, O *Wakan-Tanka.* You will be here with us!

Just as the first rays of the sun began to enter the tipi, Moves Walking picked up a stone axe, offered it to *Wakan-Tanka,* and struck the ground at the center of the sacred place which he had scraped in front of him. Then, offering the axe to the west, he struck that side of the sacred place, and in the same manner he struck the ground at the three other quarters. Then, after holding the axe to the earth, he once again struck the center.

Moves Walking took the knife and slowly scraped the earth from this place which he had marked out and placed the earth at the east; next he took up a handful of the purified earth, and, after offering a small part of it to the Power of the west, he put the earth on the western side of the sacred place. In the same manner earth was placed at the other three directions and at the center. Then, with the earth which he had piled at the east, Moves Walking made a mound at the center and carefully spread it all over the sacred place. Finally, he leveled it off with an eagle feather.

He then picked up a pointed stick and, after offering it to *Wakan-Tanka,* drew a line in the soft earth, from the west to the east; after offering the stick again to the heavens, he drew another line from the north to the south. Finally, the altar was completed by making two lines of tobacco on top of the two paths drawn on the ground, and then this tobacco was painted red. This altar now represented the universe and all that is in it. At its center was

Wakan-Tanka; His presence was really there in the altar, and that is why it was made in such a careful and sacred way.

While Moves Walking was making the sacred altar, he sang the sacred-pipe song (*Cannumpa wakan oloowan*), while another Lakota in the lodge made low and rapid thunder on the drum.

Friend do this! Friend do this! Friend do this!
If you do this your Grandfather will see you.
When you stand within the holy circle,
Think of me when you place the sacred tobacco in the pipe.
If you do this He will give you all that you ask for.

Friend do this! Friend do this! Friend do this!
If you do this your Grandfather will see you.
When you stand within the holy circle,
Send your voice to Wakan-Tanka.
If you do this He will give you all that you desire.

Friend do this! Friend do this! Friend do this!
If you do this your Grandfather will see you.
When you stand within the holy circle,
Crying and with tears send your voice to Wakan-Tanka.
If you do this you will have all that you desire.

Friend do this! Friend do this! Friend do this!
That your Grandfather may see you.
When you stand within the sacred hoop,
Raise your hand to Wakan-Tanka.
Do this and He will bestow upon you all that you desire.

There is much power in this song because it was given to us by the White Buffalo Cow Woman at the time when she brought to us our most holy pipe. This song is used even today, and it makes my heart good whenever I hear or sing it.

As Moves Walking was making the altar and singing the sacred song, a young girl who was to play an important part in the rite was brought into the tipi by her father, and, passing around the lodge sun-wise, she took her place to the left of Moves Walking. Her name was *Wsu sna win* (Rattling Hail Woman), and she was the daughter of High Hollow Horn.

Moves Walking picked up the sacred ball, which had been made from the hair of the buffalo and covered with tanned buffalo hide. He painted this ball red, the color of the world, and, with blue paint representing the heavens, he made dots at the four quarters; then made two blue circles running all around the ball, thus making two paths joining the four quarters. By completely encircling the red ball with the blue lines, Heaven and Earth were united into one in this ball, thus making it very sacred.

He then put sweet grass upon a coal, and over the smoke he purified the pipe and began to pray, holding the pipe stem to the heavens.

"O *Wakan-Tanka,* behold this pipe which we are about to offer. You we know are the first, and You have always been. We shall walk the path of life, carrying in one hand the sacred pipe which You have given us, and in the other hand will be our children. In this way the generations will come and go and will live in a holy manner. This is Your sacred day, for on this day we shall establish a rite which will complete the seven rites of the pipe. O *Wakan-Tanka,* look down upon us as we offer the pipe to You. On this day the four Powers of the universe will be with us. O You, Power, there where the sun goes down, who control the waters, we are about to offer this pipe: help us with your two good days! Help us!"

This tobacco was placed in the pipe for the West, and then pinches of tobacco representing the other Powers or directions, were put into the pipe, with the following prayers for each:

"O You where the Giant lives, who purifies with Your white breath, and You, winged one who guard this straight path, we are placing You in this pipe, and so help us with Your two sacred red and blue days!"

"O You, Power of the place where the sun comes up, and you Morning Star, who divides the darkness from the light, giving wisdom to the two-legged peoples! with You we shall offer this pipe. Help us with Your two good days!"

"O You, Power of that place where we always face, from which the generations come and go; O You, the White Swan, who guard the sacred path! there is a place for You in this pipe which we are about to offer to *Wakan-Tanka.* Help us with Your two good days!"

"O You, winged of the blue heavens; You who have strong wings and eyes which see everything—You live in the depths of the heavens and are very close to *Wakan-Tanka.* We are about to offer this pipe; help us with your two sacred red and blue days!"

"O You, Grandmother, from whom all earthly things come, and O You, Mother Earth, who bear and nourish all fruits! behold us and listen! Upon You there is a sacred path which we walk, thinking of the sacredness of all things. Upon You there will be made sacred this young and pure girl, Rattling Hail Woman, for it is she who will stand at the center of the earth, holding the *wakan* ball. Help us, O Grandmother and Mother, with Your two good days, as we offer this pipe to *Wakan-Tanka!*"

With these prayers the pipe was filled and placed against the little blue rack made of forked sticks stuck into the ground. Moves Walking then picked up the painted ball and handed it to the young girl, telling her to stand and to hold it in her left hand and to raise her right hand up to the heavens. Moves Walking then began to pray, holding the pipe in his left hand, and holding his right hand up to the heavens.

"O Grandfather, *Wakan-Tanka,* Father, *Wakan-Tanka,* behold us! Behold Rattling Hail Woman, who stands here holding the universe in her hand. Upon that earth all that moves will rejoice this day. The four Powers of the universe, and also the sacred heavens, are there with the ball—all this Rattling Hail Woman sees. The dawn of the day, and the Light of *Wakan-Tanka* is now upon her. She sees her generations to come and the tree of life at the center. She also sees the sacred path which leads from the place where You always face to there where the giant lives. She sees her Grandmother and Mother Earth and all her relatives in the things that move and grow. She stands there with the universe on her hand, and all her relatives there are really one. O Grand-

133

father, *Wakan-Tanka,* Father, *Wakan-Tanka,* it is by Your will that Your Light is now shining upon this girl. This day we all feel Your presence. We know that You are here with us. For this and for all that You have given us, we give thanks."

Moves Walking then stood before the buffalo skull and spoke to him in this manner: "*Hunka* spirit, today they have given to you a paint which I now put upon you, for you are related to our people, the two-leggeds, and it is through you that they live. After I put this sacred paint upon you, you will go forth with this young girl, and you will give of your grace to all the people."

Moves Walking then painted the buffalo by making a red line around the head, and then a straight line from between the horns to between the eyes. When he had finished this, he went and sat next to Rattling Hail Woman and spoke to her.

"Rattling Hail Woman, you are sitting there in a sacred manner! It is good, for the spirits of the buffalo have come to see you, and, therefore, I shall reveal to you the vision which I have received. In my vision I went towards the place where the Giant lives, and I saw a great people moving as if on a journey. They, too, had their guards, their chiefs, and their holy men of prayer, just as we do. And as I came before these people, they stopped and one of their leaders came forward and spoke to me.

" 'Two-legged, behold these people who are sacred! They are now going to teach an honored young one to walk, and in her life you will see four ages.'

"Then they brought forward a tiny girl, who sat down, and I saw that she was a little buffalo calf. She stood up and began to walk, but then she staggered and lay down. Her people, who I now saw were buffalo people, gathered around the little calf, and one buffalo cow snorted a red breath upon her, and when the calf lay down again I saw that she was now a white yearling buffalo. The mother continued to snort red and to nudge the yearling. When she got up again I saw that she had changed a second time, and was now a larger buffalo. The young buffalo then lay down, but when she got up again she was full grown; and then she ran away over the hill, and all the buffalo snorted, so that they shook the universe. I then saw buffalo at all the four quarters, but they were now people, and I saw the little girl standing at the center with a ball in her hand. The girl tossed the ball to the place where the sun goes down, and all the people scrambled for it and returned it to the center. In the same manner, the girl tossed the ball towards the place where the Giant lives, towards the place where the sun comes up, and then to the place towards which we always face; each time the ball was returned to the girl at the center. The last time the little girl threw the ball straight up, and immediately they all turned back into buffalo, and, of course, none of them were able to catch the ball, for the buffalo people do not have hands as we do. The little girl, who was now a buffalo calf again, took the ball and nudged it towards me, and the leader of the buffalo people then said to me: 'This universe really belongs to the two-leggeds, for we four-legged buffalo people cannot play with a ball; you should therefore take this and return to your people and explain to them that which we have taught you here.' "

Moves Walking then explained this rite to Rattling Hail Woman and to the other people gathered there: "In the buffalo there are four ages, as they have shown me in this vision. Rattling Hail Woman and the buffalo—represented by his skull—shall together go forth from this tipi, and she will throw the ball as I have explained to you in the vision. It is the will of *Wakan-Tanka* that this be done. Do not forget that the ball is the world and, also, our Father, *Wakan-Tanka,* for the world or the universe is His home; thus, whoever catches the ball will receive a great blessing. All of the people must try to catch the ball, and Rattling Hail Woman will be the buffalo calf at the center. She shall now leave, stopping four times as she goes, and each step that she takes will be for the benefit of her people."

All the people had gathered around the tipi in order to hear what was being said; they all were dressed in their best clothes, and everybody was happy. High Hollow Horn walked out of the lodge first, holding the sacred pipe, and after him followed his daughter, Rattling Hail Woman, carrying the ball in her right hand. Moves Walking then followed holding the buffalo skull, and snorting. Four times he pushed Rattling Hail Woman with the skull, and each time red smoke came out its nose. As he did this, Moves Walking sang one of his *wakan* songs.

> *In a sacred manner from all directions,*
> *They are coming to see you.*
> *Rattling Hail Woman has been sitting in a sacred*
>   *manner.*
> *They are all coming to see her!*

Finally, when they stopped the fourth time, High Hollow Horn and Moves Walking stood on either side of the girl, facing towards the place where the sun goes down. The girl then threw the ball towards the west, and one of the people there caught the ball and, after embracing it and offering it to the six directions, handed it back to the girl at the center. In the same manner, the three then faced towards the place where the Giant lives, and the ball was thrown in that direction, all the people scrambling for it, finally returning it to the center. Then the ball was thrown to the place where the sun comes up, and then to the place where we always face, and each person who was fortunate enough to catch the ball was given a horse or some valuable present. The fifth time, the ball was thrown straight up, and there was then a great scramble, until finally one person had the ball and returned it to the girl at the center.

When the throwing of the ball had been finished, High Hollow Horn offered the sacred pipe to Moves Walking, who held the stem towards the heaven and began to send a voice to *Wakan-Tanka*.

"*Hee-ay-hay-ee-ee!* [Four times]. I am sending a voice to You, O *Wakan-Tanka*—to You who have always been, and who are above all things. Father, *Wakan-Tanka*, You are the chief of all things; everything belongs to You, because it is You who have created the universe. Upon this great island You have placed our people, and You have given us the wisdom to know all things. You have made us to know the moon and the sun, the four winds

and the four Powers of the universe. We know that the generations come from, and return to, that place towards which we
always face, and upon this straight red path leading to where the
giant lives we have walked in a sacred manner. And above all, we
know that our four closest relatives are always our Grandfather
and Father, *Wakan-Tanka,* and our Grandmother and Mother,
the Earth. O *Wakan-Tanka,* behold today Rattling Hail Woman
who holds in her hand a ball which is the earth. She holds that
which will bring strength to the generations to come who will in-
herit Thy earth; and the steps that they take will be firm, and they
will be free from the darkness of ignorance. Rattling Hail Woman
stands here holding Your world, and, from this day on, this ball
will belong to the generations to come, and they will rejoice as
they walk hand-in-hand with their children. Help them to walk
the sacred path without ignorance. May the heavens above behold
us here and be merciful to us! Grandfather, *Wakan-Tanka!* Father,
Wakan-Tanka! may we always know and do Thy will. May we
never lose this relationship established here! May we cherish it
and love it always! O *Wakan-Tanka,* be merciful to me, that my
people may live!"

The sacred pipe was then smoked or touched by all who were
present, and those who were fortunate enough to have caught the
holy ball were given presents of horses or buffalo robes, and all
the people had a great feast and everybody was happy, for that
which the White Buffalo Cow Woman had promised in the beginning had now been fulfilled.

I, Black Elk, should now explain to you several things that you
may not understand about this holy rite. First, it is a little girl,
and not an older person, who stands at the center and who throws
the ball. This is as it should be, for just as *Wakan-Tanka* is eternal-
ly youthful and pure, so is this little one who has just come from
Wakan-Tanka, pure and without any darkness. Just as the ball is
thrown from the center to the four quarters, so *Wakan-Tanka* is
at every direction and is everywhere in the world; and as the ball
descends upon the people, so does His power, which is only received by a very few people, especially in these last days.

You have seen that the four-legged buffalo people were not able to play this game with the ball, and so they gave it to the two-leggeds. This is very true because, as I have said before, of all the created things or beings of the universe, it is the two-legged men alone who, if they purify and humiliate themselves, may become one with—or may know—*Wakan-Tanka*.

At this sad time today among our people, we are scrambling for the ball, and some are not even trying to catch it, which makes me cry when I think of it. But soon I know it will be caught, for the end is rapidly approaching, and then it will be returned to the center, and our people will be with it. It is my prayer that this be so, and it is in order to aid in this "recovery of the ball," that I have wished to make this book.

Hehaka Sapa (personal name): x
High Hollow Horn (personal name): 11 ff., 128 ff.
Hokshichankiya: 27, 28, 113
Humility: 26, 54 n.; symbolized by rabbit, 85
Hunkas, the hiding of: 111
Huntka: 20
Hyde, George E.: xiii

Kablaya, Spread (personal name): 67 ff.
"Keeping of the Soul" rite prohibited by government: 10 n.
Kinnikinnik: 16 n., 20, 48; observances in cutting, 50; 57

La Flesche, Francis: 21 n., 43 n.
Lamenting: 44 ff.; reason for, 45–46; for women, 46
Light, as destroyer of ignorance: 40
Little Big Horn, battle of: x
Little Warrior (personal name): xii, xiii
Lodge: construction for ceremonial, 4 n.; symbolism in sun dance,
    80; diagram of sun dance, 81

Maka (the earth): 27
Matohoshila, Bear Boy, (personal name): 101
Maya owichapaha ("She who pushes them over the bank"): 29 n.
Menstruation: 116 ff.
Milky Way: 29 n.
Minnesota: xi
Mississippi: xi
Moon, symbolism of: 71
Morning star, symbolism of: 63
Moves Walking (personal name): 128 ff.

Nature, importance to the Indian: ix
Neihardt, John G.: xiii, 5, 45 n.
Nicholson, R. A.: 75 n.

Onikare (sweat lodge): 31; *see also* purification
Osage Indians, purification rites of: 42 n.

The type used in this book is Linotype Granjon in the eleven-point size
with two points of space between lines. Extremely economical, in that
many letters are accommodated in a given line, Granjon was designed
for machine composition a quarter of a century ago by the eminent
English printer, George W. Jones. It is not a copy of a classic design,
though it owes much to the sixteenth-century types of Claude Gara-
mond. The text here is set in relatively short lines in order to provide
greater reading ease.

The decorations throughout the book are adapted from Sioux bead-
work designs, strictly geometric, and having no particular symbolic
significance, except, perhaps, to the individual Indian creators.

UNIVERSITY OF OKLAHOMA PRESS : NORMAN